# UNFU*K
# YOURSELF

## Get out of your head
## and into your life

GARY JOHN BISHOP

HarperOne
*An Imprint of* HarperCollins*Publishers*

UNFU\*K YOURSELF. Copyright © 2016 by Gary John Bishop. All rights reserved. Printed in the United States of America. No part of this book may be used or reproduced in any manner whatsoever without written permission except in the case of brief quotations embodied in critical articles and reviews. For information, address HarperCollins Publishers, 195 Broadway, New York, NY 10007.

HarperCollins books may be purchased for educational, business, or sales promotional use. For information, please email the Special Markets Department at SPsales@harpercollins.com.

Originally published as *Unfu\*k Yourself* in the United States of America in 2016 by the author.

First HarperOne hardcover published in 2017

FIRST EDITION

Designed by Rainmaker Creative

Library of Congress Cataloging-in-Publication Data

Names: Bishop, Gary John, author.
Title: Unfu\*k yourself : get out of your head and into your life / by Gary John Bishop.
Other titles: Unfuck yourself
Description: First edition. | New York, NY : HarperOne, 2017.
Identifiers: LCCN 2017025227| ISBN 9780062803832 (hardcover) | ISBN 9780062819499 (audio)
Subjects: LCSH: Self-talk. | Self-realization. | Success.
Classification: LCC BF697.5.S47 B57 2017 | DDC 158.1—dc23 LC record available at https://lccn.loc.gov/2017025227

18 19 20 21   LSC   20

This book is dedicated to my three sisters, Paula, Elizabeth, and Sandra; my mother, Agnes; and my father, Patrick. We grew together, we cried together, we stood together, and we fought together. I am who I am because of you.

I acknowledge the downbeat and downtrodden, the single mothers and unemployed fathers, the dreamers and wannabes; I am you, and you can do it.

# Table of Contents

# In the beginning...

*"This is a conversational slap from the universe to wake you up to your true potential, to unfuck yourself, and get spectacularly into your life."*

# CHAPTER 1

# Have you ever felt like a hamster on a wheel, furiously churning your way through life but somehow going nowhere?

All the while you're caught in a loop of constant internal chatter and judgement that never stops, a little voice telling you that you're lazy or stupid or not good enough. You won't even notice the degree to which you believe it or are drained by it, you'll just be spending your day working to overcome the stresses and strains, trying to live your life and at various points facing the resignation that if you can't get your ass off this damned wheel maybe you are never going to get to where you want in life—maybe that happiness you're after or that weight you want to lose or that career or relationship you crave will remain just out of reach.

These pages are dedicated to those who experience that self-defeating monologue. The endless stream of doubt and subterfuge that limits and taints everyday life. This is a conversational slap from the universe to wake you up to your true potential, to unfuck yourself, and get spectacularly into your life.

Let's get this thing started in the right place. There are two kinds of talk you engage in every day: talking to others and talking to yourself. You might be one of those who insist, "I don't talk to myself!" But, in fact, most of the conversations you have on any given day are with yourself—all "enjoyed" in the solitude and privacy of your own head.

Whether you're introverted or extroverted, creative or practical, you spend huge swathes of your time talking to . . . YOU! You do it while exercising, working, eating, reading, writing, walking, texting, crying, arguing, negotiating, planning, praying, meditating, having sex (on your own and with others)—you name it. And yes, you even do it in your sleep.

You're actually doing it right now.

Don't worry, it doesn't mean you're crazy. Or, perhaps it means we're all a little crazy. Either way, we all do it, so settle in and welcome to the freak show.

Studies show that we have over fifty thousand thoughts per day. Think of all the things you say to yourself that you'd rather not or that you try to overcome or defeat. While we have little or no say in those automatic and reactionary thoughts, we have a massive say in which of those same thoughts we attach significance to. They don't come preloaded!!

The latest in neuroscience and psychology adds weight to the idea that the *kind* of talk you engage in has a profound impact on the quality of your life. Professor Will Hart of the University of Alabama conducted four experiments in which participants either recalled or experienced a positive, negative, or neutral event. They found that people who described the neutral event in ways that suggested it was ongoing actually felt more positive and when they described a negative event in the same way, they experienced more negativity. In simple terms, the language you use to describe your circumstances determines how you see, experience, and participate in them and dramatically affects how you deal with your life and confront problems both big and small.

The connection between what we say and how we feel has been known for hundreds if not thousands of years. Philosophers like Wittgenstein, Heidegger, and Gadamer all knew of the importance and significance of language in our lives. Wittgenstein said, "The harmony between thought and reality can be found in the grammar of the language."

The good news is, studies have continually found that positive self-talk can dramatically improve mood, boost confidence, increase productivity, and more. Much more. In fact, as evidenced by Professor Hart and his studies, it can be one of the key components to a happy, successful life.

The bad news is, the reverse is also true: Negative self-talk can not only put us in a bad mood, it can leave us feeling helpless. It can make small problems seem bigger—and even create problems where none existed before. Here's the breaking news: your self-talk is fucking you over and in ways you can't even begin to imagine.

With all of this in mind, let's get one thing clear: Even though this is a book about using the right language to improve your life, I'm NOT suggesting you suddenly take on positive thinking or personal affirmations.

Those subjects have been done to death with varying degrees of success and are certainly not what we'll be doing here.

I won't ask you to tell yourself you're a tiger as a way to unleash your inner animal. Firstly, you're not a tiger and secondly, well, you're not a tiger. This all may work for some people, but I'm much too Scottish for that. To me, being told to do these sorts of things feels like being force fed a bucket of maple syrup liberally sprinkled with bits of last year's candy canes. Thanks but eh, no thanks.

For all my "positives" out there, sorry but we're taking this baby in another direction! This book is designed to give you an authentic leg up—one that feels genuine and right for you and can propel you into greater levels of your true potential.

## THE DIFFERENCE BETWEEN SUCCESS AND FAILURE

> *"If human emotions largely result from thinking, then one may appreciably control one's feelings by controlling one's thoughts— or by changing the internalized*

*sentences, or self–talk, with which one largely created the feeling in the first place."*

That quote comes from Albert Ellis, one of the forefathers of modern psychology. Ellis found that how we think and talk about our experiences shifts the way we feel about them. In short, our thoughts are bedfellows with our emotions.

Ellis also found that the way we think can often be completely irrational.

Consider how many times you've told yourself something like, "I'm so stupid," "I always mess things up," "My life is over," or some negative description of an event like, "This is the worst thing that's ever happened to me."

Raise your hand if you've ever completely overreacted to something that, in hindsight, barely registered on the important-o-meter? Okay, put your hand down, people are watching and you're starting to look a bit silly. If you look back you'll see that in the instant before that seemingly random overreaction, you had a flash of outrageous self-talk, ***BANG!*** . . . and off you go with your good self.

Some of the things we say and do aren't always particularly rational but we seem to say and do them anyway! In addition, we never really see what we are leaving ourselves with or the emotional residue of engaging in even the mildest of negative self-talk.

You see, it's not always dramatic self-talk, sometimes it's subtle but equally disempowering. If you're working on something, you might think, **"This is so hard. What if I don't finish in time?"** or worry about all the different ways you can "mess up," which leaves you in an anxious or worried state. Sometimes negative self-talk leads to anger, sadness, or frustration that manifests in different or seemingly unrelated situations.

This kind of self-talk doesn't make your life any easier. The more you tell yourself how hard something is, the harder it will actually seem. Unfortunately, since we are constantly listening to a steady stream of our automatic inner thoughts and have become so accustomed to the critical voice in our heads, we often don't realize how negative thoughts impact our mood and behavior in any given moment and, as a result, we end up doing—or not doing—things our rational minds want us to do.

For a simple example, take a moment to think about the daily chores you dread the most, all because you've built them up in your mind to be something worse than they really are. We sometimes avoid simple things like folding laundry and unloading the dishwasher, when they actually take little time and effort. With enough of these little persistent items hanging around it's easy to collapse them in with the bigger, more important things until we find ourselves overwhelmed or exhausted by life.

Why do we "resist" certain things in our lives? We have a personal conversation about those kinds of tasks that is firmly rooted in some negative opinion. Look in your own life for your "stuck-ness" and you'll see what I mean. You have a pretty serious self-talk blockage!

## HOW LANGUAGE CHANGES OUR LIVES

The way we talk doesn't only affect us in the moment. It can seep into our subconscious and become internalized, changing our thoughts and behavior in the long term.

In real everyday terms, the way we talk to ourselves and others instantly shapes how we perceive life, and that same perception directly impacts our behavior right there in the moment. Ignore your perceptions at your peril! Even worse, live with the illusion that you don't have perceptions!

If you're sometimes talking about how "unfair" life is, you'll start to act according to that view, perceiving slights where none exist or, as studies have shown, putting less effort into your work because you've already determined it won't accomplish anything. The unfair view will quickly become your reality.

On the other hand, the person who views success as if it were just around the corner will not only work his butt off to achieve it but be energized and alive to it and all the while acting on that fundamental view of success. To be clear, believing you will be successful is only one (albeit important) part of success. By the same token, there is a way to accomplish great things without that belief although the ride will be a bit rougher!

If you're worried that you don't have that kind of personal belief, READ ON!

Marcus Aurelius, the Stoic philosopher turned Roman emperor, said, "Here is a rule to remember in the future, when anything tempts you to feel bitter: not

'This is misfortune,' but 'To bear this worthily is good fortune.'"

It's entirely within our power to determine how we think about and talk about our problems. They can be a nuisance or a stepping stone. They can hold us down or lift us up.

In fact, Stoic philosophers like Aurelius believed that outside events hold no power over us at all. We create our own reality with our minds.

> *"Reject your sense of injury and the injury itself disappears."*
> *- Marcus Aurelius*

Take some time here to ponder that statement.

How willing are you to consider that your life is the way it is, not because of the weight of your circumstances or situation, but rather the weight of self-talk that pulls you down? That what you think you can and cannot do is influenced much more directly by some subconscious response than by the reality of life itself?!

If you keep looking out there (outside of yourself) to your circumstances and feverishly working to get out of them you'll keep getting the same response. No power, no joy, no vitality. At best it's a seesaw of success and

"It's not that you have to find the answer, you are the answer."

disappointment, happiness and despair. Sometimes your circumstances just don't change, sometimes they stagnate and crystalize. What if that thing you're working toward, that thing you are sure will make you happier, better, or more confident doesn't happen? What then? Even if it does arrive someday, what happens to your life between now and *that* day?

This book will require you to seek the answer, not out there, but *inside* of yourself. It's not that you have to *find* the answer, you *are* the answer. As I've said to my clients many, many times, people spend their lives waiting for the cavalry, all the while never realizing *they* are the cavalry. Your life is waiting on you to finally show up.

## RETRAIN YOUR BRAIN—ONE WORD AT A TIME

All this talk about our subconscious isn't just a bunch of psychobabble.

Scientists have discovered that our thoughts can actually change the physical structure of our brain. This phenomenon, neuroplasticity, is revolutionizing the way we think about the human mind.

As we go through life learning and experiencing new things, our brain is constantly arranging and rearranging the neural pathways that control how we think and behave. The best part is, we direct our thoughts in a way that consciously modifies these pathways for ourselves. And the easiest way to shape those thoughts is through conscious, decisive self-talk. The kind of talk that "cuts through" and takes control of your life.

Just like we build habits by repeating an action until it becomes "automatic," we can use strong, assertive language over time to create lasting change in our lives. It's more than just happy thoughts (don't break out the candy canes just yet)—you're affecting your brain's very biology.

We can determine our emotions by steering our thoughts. We can shape those thoughts by being conscious of and diligent about our words and the kind of language we engage in. A lot of this will come down to your basic tolerance of your current mindset and your willingness to change it.

It all starts by making a conscious choice to talk in a way that's helpful rather than harmful. By using the right kind of language and framing our problems in a more readily accessible light, we can quite literally change the way we see and interact with the world. All that stuff you've heard and read about "creating your own reality"? It's not only possible but millions of people the world over are already doing it! And the best part is, they're not only creating it, they are in fact acting on it and living it.

Remember, no matter how difficult, challenging, or pressing life's circumstances can be, how you fundamentally relate to and engage with those circumstances will have the biggest say in how they turn out. Again, the answer is inside you rather than outside you.

How we talk, think about, and therefore perceive our surroundings is the very foundation for our reality. Create the reality you want to live in by beginning the process of having the kind of conversations (with yourself and others) that actually shape that reality. A simple way that I reframe my own everyday "problems" is by relating to them as opportunities. They instantly become items in my life that I use to educate and expand myself. I become curious and engaged with them rather than my usual default annoyed and frustrated self!

## ASSERTIVE VS NARRATIVE

How the heck does one create their own reality?
By shifting your self-talk from being a streaming
narrative (where you talk *about* yourself, others, and
life, a dialogue of opinion and judgement), to being
**assertive**, where you cast all of the default "noise"
aside and assert your power right here and now.

One of the first mistakes we make is when we talk
about what we are *going* to do or who we *will* be.
Don't even get me started on "should" or "try"!
Subconsciously we are already determining when that
will be happening and it's certainly not in this moment
of time.

One of the reasons why we so often abandon
New Year's resolutions is because they usually use
language to describe what we are "going" to do,
i.e. later. All too often they begin with what we're
*not* going to do, which leaves us enthusiastic at
the beginning but out of juice when faced with the
inevitable moment when reality takes a swing at
your face. You'll be standing there alone in the giant
hole in your life left open by that behavior you are
apparently "stopping." Those are the moments in
life when your internal dialogue runs riot! What if

you've promised yourself to lose weight and are craving pizza or if you promised to save some money but that jacket you just can't live without is suddenly on sale? How does one deal with *those* moments when the enthusiasm wanes and those old thought patterns reemerge? What are you going to do **instead**?

Assertive self-talk is when you stake a claim for this moment of time, right here and now. When you start to talk in terms of "I am..." or "I embrace..." or "I accept..." or "I assert...," all of which are powerful and commanding uses of language rather than the narrative of "I will..." or "I'm going to..."

The physiological and psychological impact of using in-the-moment, assertive language is not only powerful, it has a very real in-the-moment effect. There's a massive difference between "I am relentless" and "I will be relentless." One of those statements intervenes in this moment of your life, the other lives more like a description of what's to come rather than what's here. All of this will require you to try out assertive speaking in your daily life and catch yourself when you're using the more general narrative kind of speaking.

## USING THIS BOOK

In this book you'll find my handpicked selection of personal assertions to empower, enliven, uplift, and embolden you to take action in your day-to-day life.

You'll also see quotes from famous historical figures, philosophers, and snippets of scientific findings, all of which are there to add weight to my approach but not to prove it. While all of this is well and good, the only real way to read and interact with this book is to explore it for yourself and try on what I am saying. Take the time to think, ponder, and experiment for yourself. There is no greater knowledge than the knowledge you have verified for yourself, in your own experience.

If you take on the following pages as a personal experiment rather than an assessment of the content, you just may end up experiencing the most radical, life-changing exercise you have ever engaged with. Some of this will confront, annoy, jar, and exasperate you. Fine, get over yourself and read on. Like a good movie, it all comes together in the end!

*If you're easily offended, stop reading now and regift this to someone in your life who you think might benefit from it.*

I hope that this book will help you understand the complexity and power of self-talk and how to use it as a force for good in your life. While we are not going to delve into the creative and destructive forces of language, you'll get a sense of the ways in which your life experiences are formed and shaped in your everyday thoughts and internal conversations.

These pages will require you to think—to cognitively connect your language and your feelings in a real and conscious way with your everyday life, to explore the vast landscapes of life that present themselves when you begin to understand the magical connection between how you speak and how you feel.

I recommend reading the book in its entirety with Post-it notes, a highlighter, or any other method you can use to flag the parts that ring your particular bell. That being said, I have designed this book to be as accessible and useful to as many people as possible. Each chapter, though part of the whole, stands on its own, so you should dip in and out of it as much as you like. Use this book up, trawl through the words for what you need to make the difference in your life until its pages are tired and weary from your appetite for change.

In the day-to-day living of your life, you probably won't need to keep poking your nose in here forever (although you might, and that's okay), so the real intention here is for you to use these ideas as a starting point whenever you are stuck or in need of rejuvenation.

At *those* times, dive right in, drink from these pages, and unleash the kind of you that the world has yet to see!

Enjoy.

# "I am willing."

*"Stop blaming luck. Stop blaming other people. Stop pointing to outside influences or circumstances."*

# CHAPTER 2

# You have the life you're willing to put up with.

Think about it. What are the problems, those heinous, dark shadows currently spoiling the warmth and happiness of your otherwise blissful life?

Do you hate your job? Are you in a bad relationship? Is there something wrong with your health? Fine, get a new job. End the relationship. Change your diet and exercise or locate the kind of help you need. Seems simple doesn't it? Even when it comes to the things you seemingly had no say in, like the death of a loved one or losing your business, you have a MASSIVE say in the ways you live your life in the aftermath of those events.

If you're not willing to take the actions to change your situation—in other words, if you're **willing to put up with** your situation—then whether you like it or not, that is the life you have chosen.

Before you think "but..." or start to get your knickers in a twist...let me say one more thing: By defending your circumstances as they are right now, you are actually **making a case** for being where you are. Give it up.

No buts. You can't afford them. They're excess baggage on a trip that requires you to travel light.

> *"Circumstances don't make the man; they only reveal him to himself."*
> *– Epictetus*

As Epictetus points out, the true measure of who you are won't be found in your circumstances but rather the way in which you respond to them. To start this new process, you must first stop another one.

> *Stop blaming luck.*
> *Stop blaming other people.*
> *Stop pointing to outside influences or circumstances.*
> *Stop blaming your childhood or neighborhood.*

This approach is fundamental to everything that I talk about in these pages. You cannot, I repeat CANNOT dwell in any blame game in your life. Even blaming yourself is completely useless. Of course you'll face situations that you seemingly can't control. You may even face tragic circumstances, like disability, disease, or the death of a loved one.

But there is *always* something you can do to impact those circumstances even if you've had them for years and still can't see a way. But first, you must be willing. To fully embrace my approach, you must first accept that while there are things that have happened in your life that you had no say in, you are 100 percent responsible for what you do with your life in the aftermath of those events. Always, every time, no excuses.

The dictionary describes willingness as "the quality or state of being prepared: Readiness."

In other words, willingness is a state in which we can engage with life and see a situation from a new perspective. It starts with you and ends with you. No one can make you willing, and you cannot move forward until you really are willing to make the next move.

When you are finally willing, you can literally experience that willingness, that innate freedom that courses through your veins, and similarly when you are not, the kind of primordial stuck-ness that halts and presses down on you like some invisible weight on your chest.

Believe me, I hear you, "I am willing but..." Every time you add the "but" to the end of that statement, you turn yourself into the victim. In my many years as a coach and mentor, I have heard as many complex life situations as there are, from the darkest of pasts to the weight and gravity of the present or crippling fear of the future; I have heard them over and over and over again. You have to hear what I am saying in the way that it's intended. I'm not saying these things to inflame you—well, maybe I am but the intention is to inflame you to your own potential, to make you realize your own greatness, not just to piss you off! Take the case, imagine for a moment, that willingness is missing in your life. Not some wispy, sheepish willingness but rather a bold willingness, the kind of willing state where you are ready for what's next and ready to act on it. Willingness to change, willingness to let go, willingness to accept. Real, magical, inspired willingness.

## FINDING THE DOOR.

*"Fate leads the willing and drags along the reluctant."*

*- Seneca*

Either you control your destiny, or your destiny will control you. Life won't stop for your pauses and procrastinations. It won't stop for your confusion or fear. It will continue right along without you. Whether you play an active part or not, the show will go on.

That's why one of the first personal assertions I teach to my clients is: **"I am willing."**

Before you can say that to yourself honestly, you must first ask yourself the question "Am I willing?" That question demands an answer. It can't just be left there in the nothingness of the universe. Am I willing? It pulls for a response. Am I willing? Its power is irresistible; I cannot escape its press for truth.

> *Am I willing to go to the gym?*
>
> *Am I willing to work on that project I've been putting off?*
>
> *Am I willing to face my social fears?*
>
> *Am I willing to ask for a raise or quit this shitty job?*

*"Life won't stop for your pauses and procrastinations. It won't stop for your confusion or fear. It will continue right along without you."*

In short, are you willing to stop living the life you have and start living the life you're after? It ALL begins with the emergence of willingness, that liquid, constantly expanding and contracting state where life springs and cedes—and all of it is within you at the flick of a linguistic switch.

We often view ourselves as procrastinators or lazy or unmotivated. When, in reality, we're simply unwilling. We put things off or avoid them completely because we tell ourselves we just don't want to do it or that we *can't* do it.

Instead of viewing this behavior as a character flaw, let's create a sense of willingness where there is apparently none. A spark of potential, if you like. You are a master generator of this state of openness and potential. Once upon a time in your life, this state was easy to access, enlivened by the vigor of youth or the curiosity of childhood. Somehow, over the years, we lost touch with this magical state.

The famous philosopher and political scientist Niccolò Machiavelli once said,

> *"Where the willingness is great, the difficulties cannot be great."*

Consider that for a second. It does not matter what you're facing in life, which obstacle you're trying to overcome—if you are willing to generate that *state* of willingness, that's your doorway to making the effort, taking the steps, dealing with the setbacks, and ultimately creating the progress and change in your life that you're seeking.

That's why such a simple statement—"I *am* willing"—is so profound. You become enlivened and empowered by its promise, open to its allure.

I ask again: Are you willing?

## WHEN THE DOOR IS CLOSED

Maybe you are, in fact, **unwilling**. In many cases, that may actually be the best answer you can give.

Sometimes declaring your unwillingness can be just as powerful as declaring willingness.

Are you willing to live with a body that's unhealthy? No. Are you willing to continue living paycheck to paycheck? No. Are you willing to put up with unworkable, unsustainable relationships? No.

## I AM UNWILLING!!

Unwillingness ignites resolve and determination. It provides an access to taking a robust and urgent approach to your situation. When you are unwilling it often represents a line in the sand where you are no longer willing to go back the way you came.

Only when you're **unwilling** to continue just simply existing, feeling unsatisfied and unfulfilled, will you make the effort necessary to make a change. Only when you're **unwilling** to put up with the bullshit any longer will you grab your shovel and start digging. At times there is no greater motivation to change than the unwillingness to do "this" any longer. Which one works for you in your life currently? "I am willing" or "I am unwilling"? Can you see how being unwilling can potentially be just as powerful as being willing?

Depending on the circumstance, some of us feel more empowered by the assertion "I am willing," while for others declaring "I am unwilling" gives them strength and resolve. You might find yourself motivated by both equally depending on the situation.

Whichever category you fall into, you can not only shift the personal assertion, you can reframe the way you approach your problems.

For example, are you willing to find a new job? Yes. "I am willing." Are you willing to stay in a job you hate? No. "I am unwilling."

Both assertions can be just as effective. It's up to you to determine which one fits your persona and situation. Which one "does it" for you?

## THE POWER OF PURPOSE

There's another way for your unwillingness to free you from the hamster wheel, because sometimes it doesn't matter what you ask yourself or how many times you've said it; you just can't muster the willingness long enough to change anything. You might well be one of life's great starters-but-not-finishers. At the end of it all, you might have to face the cold reality that you have been all too willing to remain the same. You have been unwilling to fundamentally change your life and lose that weight for good, that somewhere in there you are okay with living this way. I mean, come on, you must be or you would have changed it by now! At some level you must have some tolerance for having your life turn out like this.

That's actually okay. Getting straight with yourself about having made the decision to stay where you are can be just as powerful as the decision to move. Why? Because sometimes recognizing that you willingly put yourself in a place where you are unhappy is often all the impetus required to make an opening for real and lasting change. This has to be done without blaming yourself and turning yourself into a victim of some internal blip or character "flaw." In the moment you realize you have cognitively and systematically put yourself here, guess what? That's right, you can cognitively and systematically get yourself out! This is also the foundation of granting yourself the grace of acceptance, of embracing what has been and daring yourself to reach for an unimaginable future.

> *"He is a wise man who does not grieve for the things which he has not, but rejoices for those which he has."*
>
> *– Epictetus*

By stating and facing your unwillingness to change, you can take stock of yourself and your life and begin to create a sliver of light for you to at least start. The secret is, once you've separated the task (or whatever it is you are dealing with) from the drama of the past, you may find yourself more open to tackling it. You'll le to get past the emotional swirl and straight to the heart of the issue itself.

## REACHING FOR THE STARS WITH SHORT ARMS

Some goals simply aren't connected to our reality. Don't get me wrong, I am all for reaching for the stars and striving for things that seem impossible. For instance, we'd probably all like to be filthy rich. But are you *willing* to do what it takes to make that much money? Are you willing to work sixty, seventy, or eighty hours of your week or skip vacations to do the work that needs to get done? Are you willing to take on more responsibility and, importantly, risk it all? Have you, in reality, confronted and dealt with what becoming filthy rich might really demand of you? The seemingly endless drain on your life and mind space? Our society has produced such a headlong rush to be the wealthiest, the smartest, the prettiest, the best dressed, the funniest, or the strongest, and somewhere in there we have lost the ability to just be ourselves, free to breathe life and choose our own path rather than carry the burden of social or familial expectation. What does all that produce? Well, a lot of disappointed and unfulfilled human beings, that's for sure.

That doesn't mean you should stop pursuing amazing life goals if that's what you really want. It also doesn't mean you should let yourself stagnate and stop improving, either. There's nothing inherently wrong in working long hours and sacrificing your quality of life, and some people might be perfectly content doing so in order to make the income or get the career they want. But so many of us have actually forgotten why we are pursuing what we are pursuing in the first place.

All too often, we focus solely on what we don't have, even though deep down we don't really need it or perhaps even want it. When I lay these things out, you might be nodding your head. "He's right, I don't need to be a millionaire" or "I don't even really want six-pack abs."

Which of course is all fine until the next time you see that nice car and think, "Why don't I have that?," or when you look at the cover of a magazine and wonder, "Why don't I look like that?" or "Why aren't my clothes that nice?" Making sure we're striving for what we *really* want requires a constant check-in with ourselves. It's not a one-and-done deal.

If you really want those things, then go get them! Begin today, lay out your strategy, deal with your reality, and, most importantly, take the actions required and take them often!

But if you're not willing to work an extra ten or twenty hours a week just to drive to work in a BMW instead of a Honda, give up the complete waste of precious headspace to yearn for it. Stop pretending to yourself. Deal with your unwillingness to take on the kind of actions accomplishing those things would require and accept that you have been bullshitting yourself. You'll have a lot more capacity for loving the life you do have and create some room to begin striving for the things you actually want in life.

"I am unwilling" to give up all of my favorite foods just to have the body I did when I was twenty. "I am unwilling" to trade time with my family for an extra zero on my paycheck.

Face your reality. Once you adopt the mindset of "I am unwilling," you will no longer be filled with guilt, resentment, or regret every time you see something you think you "want." You'll be in a place where you are connected to and in tune with your real life and, if you really want to pursue those things in the future, you'll be able to locate yourself from that reality and plot your road to accomplish them.

## CHART YOUR PATH

One of the beautiful things about really taking a hard look at your life and goals is that doing so forces you to reevaluate the path that leads to them.

Is exercising thirty minutes a day *really* as impossible as your mind has built it up to be? Sure, you're going to get a little sweaty and tired but you can throw on your favorite music to help the time go by faster. And, even though it might start out painfully, you'll eventually get used to that and grow stronger.

What's the worst thing that can happen if you offer your idea in that meeting? It gets shot down? So what? Even if you're faced with bigger tasks—MUCH bigger tasks like years of back taxes, a hoarder's paradise of a garage, telling the truth to someone you've been lying to—the path to change starts with that same glimmer of willingness.

Bear in mind we all tend to build things up in our minds to be a lot bigger than they really are. Telling the truth becomes a trek to the Sahara Desert and back. If that's the case for you, try breaking the task down into smaller declarations of willingness to "stand up," "get out of bed," "open my email," etc.

Of course you might well be dealing with something much bigger than these examples but even when you ramp it up, the same model works exceptionally well. Let's say you have been holding on to a dark secret. Maybe you're ashamed or guilty or resentful. Perhaps this is something that could change your life in a significant way. "Am I willing to tell the truth to that person I've been lying to?" When you frame it this way, coming clean becomes an occasion to talk, listen, and then deal with the consequences. You might be dreading it but you can do it. It's not the task that's important, it's the life that's available *after* that's at stake here. When you are free to be open and available, with nothing held back, no lies, no withholds or half-truths, you really are your most expressive, most alive self.

Most of the time, the task we're actually facing is a lot simpler than we think it is. The problem is, we usually don't take the time to really look at it. Some of the things we face certainly can be challenging, but at the same time what's on the other side of those challenges is a life of our dreams. A life where we are willing and open and inspired to take it on.

Make that assertion, "I am willing."

## PLANT YOUR FLAG

When you start to view the world through the lens of what you're willing and unwilling to pursue, rather than what it seems you want and don't want, things start to become a lot clearer.

Instead of wasting time worrying about the things other people have, you'll start focusing on what's really important to you and your life. You'll realize that once you replace envy, lust, and desire with a willingness to change your life for the better, things really start to take shape.

When we understand what we are genuinely willing to do, we take back control over the subconscious thoughts and feelings that previously directed our behavior away from where we truly wanted to go. You have the ability to determine what your truth is, and not from some subconscious glitch that keeps popping up from the past, either, but instead from your cognitive and conscious self, from the power of intervening on behalf of yourself. Willingness is a truth, a true beauty that only you can generate. No longer will thoughts like "I am a failure because I'm not a millionaire" or "I am lazy because I'm not a size 6" have the power to make you feel like crap because you will have owned your choices. Once you frame the obstacles in your life as a matter of "willing" and "unwilling"—instead of weighing yourself down with negative opinions of yourself and your circumstances—you can break through the self-imposed barriers that are truly holding you back. You can see through the distractions of self-talk and drama.

You'll realize that when you're willing to do what it takes, nothing else matters. You won't put off the things you're truly willing to do. You won't neglect the responsibilities you took on because you will feel the strong sense of willingness to do them.

Willingness. It's the lifeblood of the new, the infinite well of possibility and potential, a state where new futures arise and a whole new you can begin.

Ask yourself "Am I willing?" over and over until you can hear it, first thing in the morning, last thing at night, while you're driving, while in the shower, "Am I willing?" Ask, ask, ask until a resounding YES echoes through your consciousness. I AM WILLING!

I ask you again, "Are you willing?"

# "I am wired to win."

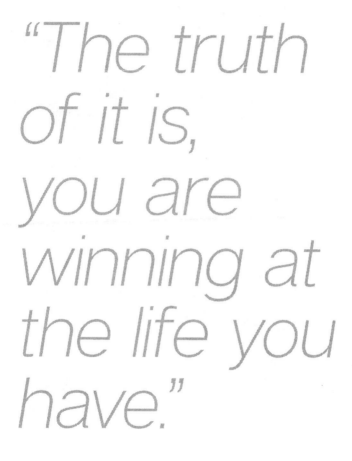

"The truth of it is, you are winning at the life you have."

# CHAPTER 3

What if I told you that even when you think you're losing in life, you're actually winning? That **everything** that happens is really a victory?

It's true. And that's not just some feel-good self-help mumbo jumbo or a sales line that I'm feeding you.

You are a champion. You've knocked out goal after goal, cruising to an undefeated record. Everything you set your mind to comes true.

You're probably starting to think I've lost my mind or maybe even that you've lost yours! Perhaps you're convinced I'm talking to someone else—anyone *but* you. Let me explain before we both end up like a couple of basket cases.

Imagine this scenario: For what seems like all of your life you've been searching for love, that one special person to share your life with. But up to this point, it hasn't happened. (Remember, this is an example, you can use any area of your own life where you have experienced being stuck in a cycle.) You've met people, had relationships, but all of them ended somewhere short of "forever." You and "the one" just never materialized. The fairy tale inevitably came to an end, often a very familiar kind of end.

After a while, you start losing hope. You start to wonder whether you will ever meet the person of your dreams. Maybe you and relationships just aren't *meant* to be?

> *Will anyone ever love me?*
> *Am I worthy of being loved?*
> *Why do I always seem to attract the same types of people?*

You look back at your childhood, to times when you didn't feel loved enough. Or periods of adolescence where you felt like an outsider or past relationships that played out like a scene from the movie *Groundhog Day* except with different players each time. So frustrating!

Then one day, you meet someone. You go on a few dates and find out you really enjoy each other's company. Things are coming along nicely as the days stretch into weeks and the weeks into months.

Eventually that day comes when you can't help yourselves—you exchange your first "I love yous."

Not only are you in love, but you start to wonder, "Could *they* be 'the one'?!" Could this be it? Wheeeeee!!! The bliss, excitement, and possibility are invigorating and enlivening.

At some point, however, the dark clouds of doubt start rolling in; it starts in small ways that grow first slowly and then all at once until the storm finally breaks loose. No sooner are you "in love" than you start to fall out, waaaaaaay out. The smallest things turn to arguments. The chemistry slowly evaporates until your relationship is a desert, barren and dry, and you are left with the soul-destroying basics of just trying to get along. Ugh. Not again.

At some point you both can see it's not working—
perhaps you reach a breaking point and have one (or
a number) of those nasty fallings-out. Maybe it just
slowly dies until you eventually decide to pull the plug.
Either way, you eventually go your separate ways. Oh
well. You're hurt, crushed but somehow resolute that
eventually things will turn out for you. Someday.

Except they *did*. Even though it may look and feel like
a loss, this was in fact a glorious, resounding win. A
victory from the Gods. HURRRAH!

The truth of it is, you are winning at the life you *have*.

**What if I don't want this life?** Fine; but this is the one
you're currently winning at.

## BUILDING THE MYSTERY

How could I possibly call a failed relationship a win?

Well I'm not about to tell you how you're better off
without certain people in your life. I'm not going to
assure you that you're a special little snowflake who
will find the perfect person "when you're ready."
I'm not going to buy into the self-righteous bumper
stickers and Internet memes that tell you how great

you are and that everyone else is the problem. You and I both know that when it comes down to it, that's just not accurate.

Nope. You won at that failed relationship because you achieved exactly what you set out to accomplish in the first place. From the very first "hello." "But, but, but my partner wasn't stepping up, THEY ruined it!" I got that but what if you subconsciously picked that person in the first place? The kind of ideal character to re-create the same vignettes of life over and over and over?

What if you are actually driven to prove the notion that no one will ever love you? What if it was planted there as a subconscious reaction to a turbulent childhood, bad breakups, or the like? And what if, with this pattern buried deep in your subconscious, you actively and deliberately undermined the success of your own relationship?

You became sensitive to problems where there were apparently none. You started picking at, getting annoyed by, and blowing up the tiniest of things. Over time you proved your point and the relationship reached its obvious, final, and natural conclusion. What if *this* is what you have become wired to win at?

You were convinced you weren't worthy of a loving relationship, so you systematically set out to prove it and you succeeded. Congratulations!

If you think this is starting to make you sound like a hopeless sadomasochist, don't worry. There is a silver lining in all of this.

You may not relate to the example I described above. Maybe you're happily married to the love of your life. Or perhaps you're beating off eligible suitors with a giant stick. Look at your own "dark spots," the parts of your life where you are most ineffective, where it seems like you *have* lost or are currently losing.

You see, our thoughts are so powerful that they are constantly pushing you toward your goals, even when you don't realize what those goals actually are! Your brain is wired to win.

It doesn't just apply to your relationships. This dynamic is at play in your career, your fitness, your finances, and everything else you do. You are hardwired to win.

That brings us to our next assertion: ***"I am wired to win."***

You're always winning because your brain is wired to. The trouble comes when what you really want—on a

*"For the most part, you're basically on autopilot, mindlessly gouging your way through life's predictable, muddy field."*

subconscious level—and what you say you want are different, sometimes radically so.

## RULER OF YOUR DOMAIN

In his research, Dr. Bruce Lipton, the famous stem cell and DNA scientist, found that 95 percent of what we do in our day-to-day life is controlled by our subconscious. Think about that for a moment. That means that out of all the things you say or do, only a tiny fraction of them are with a true sense of volition.

Think of all those times you lost track of time, drove home and couldn't remember a single thing about the journey, or forgot what day it was. For the most part, you're basically on autopilot, mindlessly gouging your way through life's predictable, muddy field.

The path you follow through life is the one dictated by your deepest, most inconspicuous thoughts. Your brain is constantly pushing you along that path, whether it's the one you would consciously choose to take or not.

Can't seem to increase your income? Can't seem to lose weight? Have you considered the subconscious, concealed beliefs about your income and your weight that may be driving your action (or lack of it)? You automatically relate to yourself as belonging to a certain economic class, with a certain level of fitness, and your actions serve to keep you in place, right where you're most familiar to yourself.

I like to say that we win in domains or worlds. Let's say you make $30,000 per year. That's a domain. All of the planning, strategy, and thinking you do to make that money constitute that domain.

Believe it or not, it's not necessarily any harder to make $60k than it is $30k. You may think it is, but that's not an absolute. Whether you work for $25 per hour or $50 per hour, forty hours of work is still forty hours of actual work. While it's important to identify what you're at work on and whether you are being productive instead of just busy, sometimes it really is a question of getting yourself into another domain. How does one do that? Firstly, you have to uncover and realize the ways in which you have limited yourself. The kind of "absolutes" that you are currently unaware of. In short, the conclusions that you have come to about yourself, others, and life itself. Those conclusions are the limit of your potential. It's only when you have broken through those conclusions and can experience a life outside of your current existence that you start to understand the power of this phenomenon.

While I appreciate that seems like an overly simplistic view of life, it's a view that can open you up to whole other worlds of accomplishment—although that's a conversation for another time. In this instance, take the case that your life is split up into particular domains that you are existing in and winning at.

The point is, you're winning in whichever domain you are playing in. You're wired to win in that domain. What it takes to move out of that domain is going to require some significant changes to your automatic.

## FIND YOUR WINNING EDGE

Still not convinced? It's time to turn the mirror on yourself and find out exactly where your wins are coming from.

Look at your problem areas. Where in your life are you struggling most? Is it your career? Is it a negative habit? Is it your diet?

Maybe you're constantly putting off work until the last minute. You'll wait and wait until you absolutely can't wait any longer, then bust out the project once the pressure of a strict deadline is looming over you.

We are always winning at proving something. In the case above, you win at proving either you have no time or that you are a procrastinator or a loser by getting things done at the very last minute. Or maybe it's something else. The key here is to question yourself, to look at your actions. What is the real point of all of this? What is it that you get to be right about when all is said and done?

Just like I demonstrated in the opening example about a romantic relationship, we hold a certain belief about ourselves or life that we prove right time and time again through our everyday actions. Those beliefs uncannily turn out to be deadly accurate in our reality. Spinning your wheels? What are you out to prove there?

"I'm not worthy of love," "I'm not smart," "I'm a failure," "I'm not as capable as I used to be." With these kinds of repeats stuck in your subconscious, is it any wonder that you are masterful in consistently proving them right? To succeed in another, more positive way, you'd have to prove those firmly held beliefs WRONG! For your persona, that's a ground-shaking idea that is almost too much to bear. It would in fact unsettle the very foundations of who you have become!

Many of my clients, I have found, have one particular thing in common: the subconscious desire to prove that their parents did a bad job raising them. This can manifest in so many different ways, some being worse than others. Some are subtle, others obvious, while all are very potent.

You might try to prove that your parents failed to raise you well by treating your body like crap, getting arrested, becoming addicted to drugs or alcohol, dropping out of school, consistently failing in relationships, encountering chronic financial crises, or any one of a number of seemingly random paths we get ourselves lost in. They can drop all the way down to simply being disconnected or lost in the pressures of work as an adult.

All of these are real-life examples that some of my clients discovered about themselves that ultimately "proved" that one or both of their parents failed to do their job, that their experiences as children did not adequately prepare them for adulthood. This belief, conveniently, also allows for a ready-made explanation as to why they did what they did and why they, from time to time, acted like complete assholes to others in *their* life.

Can you see ways in which you do this in your own life? Think of the problem areas in your life. Now think about them in terms of what you are winning at. What do you see there?

If you're struggling to get work done, perhaps you believe that you're incapable or lazy. You prove that idea every single time you pause or procrastinate. You're proving to yourself and others that you really are that person. Why do we do such things? We are survival machines and what better way to survive what's to come than by reliving what has been? After all, it got you this far regardless of how bad or negative it has been. You have survived.

Don't limit yourself to the examples I'm giving. They're just that: examples. You could be winning at something completely different. Take some time for introspection. If need be, write down the patterns you are seeing. Put the pieces of the jigsaw together.

Maybe you had great parents but still find yourself incapable of committing to one person. Could it be because you believe your significant other couldn't possibly live up to the example you were raised with?

The point is we all have these items.

Search out and connect all the different situations that came into play in your life. Take note of all the times you broke your promise to diet, save your money, or speak your mind. Consider how many days you skipped the gym. Think about how you went to the mall instead of the bank. Pick one and see if you can discover the "win." The amount of times you argued or lost your temper when you know you shouldn't have. What is it all pointing to?

Whatever the domain you're winning in, you'll start to realize something—you're really good at it.

You can avoid those dirty dishes in the sink for days. You use every plate, cup, and piece of silverware in the house and then you start getting creative until you're eating cereal out of a handy Tupperware container using a wooden baking spoon. Holy crap, a life hack, take a picture and get it on your Pinterest page!

It's actually rather impressive in a weird kind of way.

Once you've taken the time to analyze your own life through this lens, you'll start to see that what I'm saying is true. You really are wired to win. You really can (and do) achieve the things you set your mind to.

The Stoic philosopher Seneca once said,

> *"It is the power of the mind to be unconquerable."*

Right now, your mind is unconquerable when it comes to proving that you're not worthy of love, that you're lazy, or that you'll always be out of shape or never have any money.

But if we change our thinking a little, we can use our mind's unconquerable nature to act on all the positive goals and dreams we hold for ourselves. *We are wired to win*—we just have to point ourselves in the right direction so we can win at something we consciously choose.

## CREATING A GAME PLAN

> *"The happiness of your life depends upon the quality of your thoughts. Therefore, guard accordingly, and take that you entertain no notions unsuitable to virtue and reasonable nature."*
>
> *- Marcus Aurelius*

We've talked about the enormous role our subconscious plays in everything we do. Even if we consciously made the right decisions at every opportunity, it would still only account for a fraction of our daily life.

The personal assertion "I am wired to win" will support you in realizing how truly powerful you and your mind are. But you still need a game plan.

That means we have to start filling our "bucket" with the right ideas. Here's a good way to start.

Think about the thing or things you'd like to change in your life. They could be related to the problem areas you looked at earlier, or they could be something completely different.

Where would you really like to see progress? What do you really want to accomplish?

Take that goal and break it down. What exact steps do you need to take to achieve it? What are the mile markers you need to set out to identify your progress?

If you want to lose weight, think about how you'll need to change your diet, get more exercise, and generally adopt more healthful, nurturing habits. Go through the daily kind of actions you'll need to practice. Get it in reality.

Don't stop there. Consider the changes in mindset you'll need to make during and after your quest to become more fit. You have to be relentless in the pursuit of your goal, particularly when those automatic past-based conversations start to become louder in your head.

Once you've faced your problems head on, how will your sense of self change? When you're the fit and healthy person you want to be, how will your beliefs about yourself be different? What will *that* life look like? I would warn against the idea that you'll suddenly be awesome. Your future is not the answer to your present.

As we've discussed, subconscious thoughts are deeply ingrained in your psyche, so it can take a lot of thinking, imagination, and commitment to transform these invisible yet powerful thoughts into ones that better align with your stated goals. As with every page here, make the time to take your time.

If you look at the problem areas you came up with before, you might be able to connect to an emotionally charged event somewhere in your life that helped set them in your mind, perhaps in the form of infidelity in a relationship, childhood bullying, parents that never quite lived up to your wants and needs, public embarrassment, or major career failures.

But the more you think about your future and what you really want to accomplish, the deeper those thought processes will work their ways into your mind and take hold. Remember, when you explore and discover what it is you've really been winning at, it's not about fighting against or resisting those thoughts and actions but rather changing direction and setting yourself new goals and outcomes. This must be the kind of work that raises your awareness and throws up red flags for when you are getting off course. The better you understand your patterns the better shot you have in altering them.

When you have set out the goals that you are claiming as yours in life and, more importantly, relentlessly taking the actions to produce, it's only a matter of when.

We are wired to win. You are wired to win. Define your game, embrace the challenge, and strive to understand yourself in deeper and more meaningful ways.

True understanding of yourself and your personal constraints allows for ever-unfolding degrees of freedom and success. The more aware you become of your hardwiring, the more space and opportunity become available in those areas.

Step out there. Trust yourself, give yourself fully to your vast capacity for victory. Set yourself the challenge of winning in new and exciting ways. Demand your greatness of yourself and repeat after me: "I am wired to win."

# "I got this."

"Everyone has their problems, and life isn't always perfect. It never will be."

# CHAPTER 4

# Ugh.

There comes a time in all of our lives when we're feeling a little down, a little defeated. When it seems like nothing is going our way. It's not like we've completely given up (although sometimes we have), but at the same time, the struggle is very real.

You could be facing a massive problem: You got laid off, your spouse filed for divorce, you wrecked your car, or maybe all three at the same time. So much for that lucky charm, huh?

Or it could be something less serious: You lost your favorite shirt. Your glasses broke. Your dog used your mail for a toy. You didn't get much sleep last night. You burned dinner.

The thing is, the negative experiences we have rarely stay contained to that one issue. They **spread**. Like a toxic chemical, they seep into all aspects of our lives.

If you're having financial trouble, you'll either consciously or subconsciously stress about it at dinner, which means you don't enjoy your meal. You start feeling on edge around family. You feel resentful toward your spouse and distant from your children. You're annoyed when your dog barks or when your neighbors make too much noise. Little things like traffic and long lines begin prompting your frustration.

It's like our *whole* life is tainted, as our smaller problems leak into the bigger picture. Like a coffee spill on your desk, small problems quickly spread and create bigger ones. As the brown liquid relentlessly heads for your laptop, phone, and stack of bills while you hopelessly pad at the random chaos with your napkin in some forlorn attempt at denying the disaster, it even creates a bigger mess.

That little mess can influence all areas of your life until your emotions surrounding that one area become the lens through which you see everything.

You end up thinking...

*Life is too hard.*

*I'll never make it through this.*

*Everyone's a jerk.*

*I'm done with this s\*\*\*.*

These sentiments don't reflect reality (no matter what you might currently think), but rather your perception of your reality. Unfortunately, knowing this makes no difference whatsoever when you're stuck right bang in the middle of it all. And, of course, all of this only makes things somehow even worse. A negative experience of myself and/or my life doesn't help me overcome what I'm dealing with, let alone enjoy my life.

To deal with this, we need to shift how we view our problems and the world and adopt a new, powerfully optimistic and grounded approach.

That's why my next personal assertion is, **"I got this."**

## PUTTING PROBLEMS IN PERSPECTIVE

*"If all our misfortunes were laid in one common heap whence everyone must take an equal portion, most people would be*

*content to take their own and depart."*

*– Socrates*

Everyone has their problems, and life isn't always perfect. It never will be. It wasn't 2,400 years ago, when Socrates was around, and it certainly isn't today.

But if we're being brutally honest with ourselves, we'll realize that our own problems are pretty insignificant compared to the rest of the world's. Really. Think about it.

If you're reading this, chances are your life isn't as hard as that of a child in Somalia or an Untouchable in India. Chances are your problems are pretty small in comparison to the ones people had when Socrates was born in 470 BC, before modern medicine or electricity or cars or any one of a number of everyday advances we take for granted in our day and age.

You don't even have to travel across the globe or back in time for a comparison, either. Travel to the other side of your town or look around your office or neighborhood, and you're almost guaranteed to find plenty of people with problems worse than yours. You might not see it but it's the same for all of us. We only see the highlight reels of others' lives while

*"Get connected to your reality, your real life instead of your emotionally soaked self-talk narrative about your life."*

being continually reminded of our own behind the scenes.

If you're rolling your eyes and wondering, "How does any of that help me solve my problems?" I'll tell you: it doesn't. None of this will change the tire on your car for you or deposit another thousand dollars into your bank account.

Now, just for a moment of your significant existence, stop picking fluff out of your belly button and look around you. Get connected to your reality, your real life instead of your emotionally soaked self-talk narrative about your life.

What this will do is help you put things in some kind of reality-based perspective. This will serve to help you face life and all of its problems with a powerful attitude, to starve the creeping specter of negativity that can and does catch us in its grip. If *everyone* around you is dealing with their issues—even those that are worse than yours—then you certainly can.

But I get it. Even as I say all of this, we both know that when disaster strikes, it's challenging to stay levelheaded. Our problems are still real, they still hurt, and they can still result in our emotions getting the better of us.

When you start having those crappy feelings, take a step back. Way back. No, back further than that, MUCH further than that. Keep going . . . see if you can picture your life for what it really is.

You have to start here with your imagination.

Firstly, I advise my clients to start by looking at their entire life. Imagine it in front of you like a railroad track, running to the left and right as far as the eye can see.

Of course, the tracks aren't just sitting in the middle of a void. They cut through countryside and cities, under tunnels and over bridges, across stretches of ocean, around towering mountains and plunging canyons. Picture the magnitude and magical variety of the surroundings.

Now look waaaay down those tracks to the left. This is your past. This is where you came from, the ground you've already covered in your journey through life.

Follow the tracks down and far into the distance. As you walk, you'll see your entire life—everything that's ever happened to you—expanding in front of you.

Take the time to think about the most memorable experiences from your life.

Perhaps you recall walking down the aisle with the love of your life. Maybe it's the birth of your first child and the feeling of holding them in your arms. Would you trade that for anything?

Go back to that family vacation you took in the Caribbean, spending a few days in paradise.

How about when you closed on your first house? Or when you landed that job you wanted? Whatever your past, savor the memory of each wonderful experience.

Depending on where you are today, you've got dozens or hundreds of great experiences to look back on. Graduations, promotions, awards, parties, and relationships. Even the little things like childhood memories that cradle and comfort you, or those memorable tastes, sights, and sounds that embrace you in their familiarity and inspire feelings of warmth and joy. Open up and allow yourself the good grace of those times.

But don't just limit it to the sugary goodness either. Think about the bad, too.

Recall all the times when you struggled, suffered setbacks, or got knocked down. The arguments, the breakups, the speeding tickets, or the late bills.

Do you remember that time when your parents caught you sneaking out and grounded you? If you experienced a tough childhood, let all of that in here. How about the time you forgot to pay your electricity bill and you had to spend the night reading by candlelight?

Or when you got surgery and had to spend days lying in a hospital bed? Or when you broke up with someone and felt depressed for weeks? Let all of it in, from the most tragic and traumatic to the merely irritating, annoying, or regretful.

Remember all the problems you faced—and eventually overcame. A lot of them may be very similar to what you're dealing with today.

You probably felt a lot of the same emotions back then, too. You thought you'd never get over your ex, that you'd never find a better job, or that you wouldn't live through the humiliation of some situation.

But you did. You raised up and kicked on and, looking back, some of those problems might even seem a little silly now.

Can you believe how upset you were when you got a D on your math test in high school? Or how bad you felt when you never got a second date with that girl or guy you liked?

Even the more serious problems probably seem a lot different today. After all, you did make it through them, and they ultimately helped shape and form who you are today.

## LOOKING TO THE FUTURE

Now that you've traveled to the end of the track in one direction, it's time to turn around and head the other way.

To the right—if you haven't figured it out—is your future. Here's where you'll find the things to come, all of the experiences and events awaiting you in life.

New relationships with people you've yet to meet. Places to visit that you've never been. Doing the things you've always wanted to try.

You'll get to experience the spine-tingling rush that comes when you first kiss someone you're really attracted to. Or the connection, satisfaction, and peace of growing old with the person you love.

Maybe you'll have children and watch them grow up, make the honor roll, score touchdowns, and perform in the school play. In no time at all they'll be introducing you to the love of *their* life. And then will come trips to the movies or Disney World with your grandkids.

There are reams of untapped potential and opportunity waiting in your future—whether it's a major life event or a night of laughing with your best friends. The future can have truly great things in store for you.

Of course, it won't all be puppies and rainbows, but you already know that. There will be trials and tribulations. Disappointments, defeats, fights, and fears. Don't stop there, keep looking ALL the way to the end, the ultimate end. That's right, this life will come to a close, your life force will cease to exist on this physical plane, your experience of being you will conclude: think about the day you're going to die. I know it's not pleasant, but it's going to happen, so why not accept it now?

In this life, you'll sometimes have to do things you don't want to, with people you don't like, and in places you don't care for. People will leave your life as quickly and easily as they come into it. You'll lose money, things will break, and your dog will die.

But you'll get through it all, the good and the bad, just like you did in the past. You'll stand there like the champion you are because they're all just yet another passing scene in the movie that is your life's story.

## A SEA OF SOMETHINGS

*"It is during our darkest moments that we must focus to see the light."*
*– Aristotle*

The purpose of this exercise is to get you to start putting things back into perspective. As you examine all the things you've experienced and all the things you've yet to experience, take a moment to examine what you are currently dealing with today. Everything on your plate at this point in time is just **another something in a sea of somethings.**

Your boat hasn't and won't sink so easily. There may be some waves, you might go through some storms, and you'll probably end up seasick from time to time, but your journey across that ocean we call life will continue.

But just like a captain facing a major squall, you can't just let yourself be tossed about. You have to step up and steer your life back in the direction you want it to go. So your journey wasn't as smooth as you wanted it to be. Does that mean you're just going to let yourself get blown off course? I didn't think so. And you definitely shouldn't let what happens in one area of life affect your outlook on the whole. You just can't afford to allow your struggles at work to make you miserable at home or let your relationship troubles affect your mood at the office.

Face your problems as they come, one by one; give them the attention they need and move on. Bundling them all together into a morass of confusion and letting them overwhelm you just won't help. It takes precision, patience, and discipline of thought. Work through each item pragmatically and with a solution in mind. Remember, *everything* is solvable, and if you can't see a solution, it only means you haven't worked it out yet.

Often the reason you can't see the solution is because you're too close to the problem. Zoom out a little, zoom out a LOT and look at the big picture. This is a phenomenon similar to what psychologists call "cognitive restructuring"—shifting the way in which your problems are presenting themselves in your life.

Our minds naturally play tricks on us, twisting and distorting our thoughts in ways that are not always rational. Even though we'd like to think we're always logical, we're not. We're at the mercy of cognitive biases, emotions, and misconceptions and most of it is completely unseen by us.

Sometimes we're too close, too involved in it to even realize. It's up to us to slow down, take a step back, and understand what's really going on.

> *"That's one of the peculiar things about bad moods—we often fool ourselves and create misery by telling ourselves things that simply are not true."*
>
> *– David D. Burns*

And if things are still out of focus, take another step back. And another. And another.

Ask yourself what's *really* going on here? until you experience your problems cleanly, clearly, and free of that emotional anchor. Persist until you can see the whole course of your life and realize that your current problems are just another bump in the road.

## YOU GOT THIS

When you've finally put things into perspective, you'll come to your assertion: "I got this." You'll start to really believe it, experience it, and live *from* it.

You can handle this. It's not going to kill you. Your life isn't over. You've got plenty more left in the tank. Plenty.

"I got this" doesn't mean you have the perfect solution. It just means you have your hands on the wheel, you have a say in this just like you've had a say all along. I mean come on, you *live* for this shit!

It's not always pretty. It's not always fun but you've got this. We're not just saying this to paper over the cracks or to make you feel a little better for a split second. Look at your track record; you've *really* got this! You'll make it work, just like you always have. You had it then and you got it now.

Get in touch with who you **really** are and say it.

I got this. I got this. I got this.

# "I embrace the uncertainty."

"Uncertainty is where new happens."

# CHAPTER 5

# You're an addict.

You're out of control and so dependent on your drug of choice, you don't even realize how it's affecting your life. You have a gnawing craving and that craving is for prediction.

Will it rain tomorrow? How will my stock perform? Who will win the Super Bowl? You're constantly looking ahead, trying to figure out what's going to happen before it actually does.

Why?

Certainty. We seek the certain and avoid the uncertain. We want to know what to expect, where to go, and what to wear. We want to be prepared. We want to be safe. It's far beyond a want though; it's more like that addiction. We're sizing people up before we even know them, predicting their character in seconds. We buy goods and brand names we're used to even though there are plenty of alternatives. We take supplements and vitamins to prevent an illness we don't yet have, date people for months, sometimes years, to make *sure* of our future, to make sure that it turns out in a way that we can predict. Give me that certainty, certainty, certainty!!

We all know the bumper stickers and internet memes that praise risk takers and urge us to embrace uncertainty. We even know that our openness to taking risks directly correlates with our potential for fortune and possibility, yet many of us still stay inside our own little organized, certain world.

And there's a reason for that. Until fairly recently, the world was a much scarier place for the likes of you and me. Every step into the unknown was a dance with death. Life was one big game of Russian roulette. Literally every day, you and every other being on the face of the earth would have been an entrée on the dinner menu for an assortment of beasts and creatures or among the poor suckers who walked blindly into the path of Mother Nature's dark sense of humor.

Lucky for us, the world isn't nearly as scary as it was thousands of years ago (although not quite a utopian safe-zone). Life has become much safer, unbelievably so, in fact. Medicine and technology get better by the day; violent crime, although rampant in our news outlets, is in fact a rarity in the everyday life of your average citizen in a Western country.

Sure, there are still deadly diseases and the threat of random acts of violence or catastrophe, but the chances of you catching a mystery zombie virus or being swept up with Dorothy and Toto to a fantastical Hollywood dreamland are, I'm happy to say, slim.

Here's some other startling news: chances are you're not going to suddenly die on the way to the grocery store, your boss isn't *actually* going to kill you if you ask for a raise, and, believe it or not, asking someone out will not result in your pants mysteriously falling to the floor, painfully exposing your SpongeBob SquarePants underwear and bringing about your early demise via acute terminal embarrassment with the insidious laughter of everyone in Starbucks ringing in your ears as you depart this mortal coil.

In other words, our aversion to risk, which was once necessary, no longer is. Those same survival instincts that once kept us alive can now be the very thing that keeps us from actually living.

## A PARADIGM OF POTENTIAL

Our obsession with certainty can be tragic and counterproductive for two reasons.

First, uncertainty is where things happen. Uncertainty is your personal pathway to opportunity. It's the environment in which you grow, experience new things, and produce new, unprecedented results. Uncertainty is where *new* happens.

> *"The desire for safety stands against every great and noble enterprise."*
>
> - *Tacitus*

When you stick to what you're comfortable with, doing the same things you've always done, you're in effect living in the past—not moving forward. You're repeating things and behaviors that at one time in your life were risky since you didn't know what they would lead to, but have since turned into routine.

Think about it: How can you go to new places if you never leave the house? How can you make friends and start romances without meeting new people? How can you do anything new by doing what you've always done?

You can't. The truth is you can't even predict what the people you know will do, let alone the people you don't know. Whether it's the checkout line or a nightclub or the bank, social situations are inevitably filled with uncertainty. Jeez, half of the time you can't even predict your own thoughts and feelings! Think of the many times you've rushed to judge and then later changed your mind.

How will you ever get a raise if you don't take the risk of asking? How will you get ahead in your career if you're always holding on to certainty and comfort?

You won't. Success is never certain. It never comes without risk. Even if you're the smartest or the hardest working, there's no guarantee of anything.

The people who go on to do great things in their lives know this. They also embrace it.

> *"In any moment of decision, the best thing you can do is the right thing, the next best thing is the wrong thing, and the worst thing you can do is nothing."*
> *– Theodore Roosevelt*

Reflect on that Teddy Roosevelt quote for a minute here. Missing the target isn't the worst thing you can do. Not taking the shot is.

You may look at successful people and think they've always had it figured out. Many of them seem to have a kind of confidence, charisma, or talent that makes everything they do seem easy. They certainly seem to have something you don't, but believe me, their rise to the top was anything but certain or easy. Most of them doubted it every single day, sometimes hundreds of times per day. That's right, they sat there, just like you are right now, wondering how they would make it, whether it was all worthwhile or whether they had what it takes.

There were days when they doubted what they were doing. Where they thought, "This is never going to work." Many found themselves on the verge of giving up at numerous occasions along the way.

They didn't succeed because they were certain they were going to succeed; they succeeded because they didn't let uncertainty stop them. They did it anyway. They ignored their doubts and kept pushing forward. They were relentless when the only thing they had to fuel them was relentlessness.

Give some thought to all the people who have achieved something great, only to quickly fade into obscurity. I'm sure you can think of a few, whether they're entertainers or business people or athletes.

In my career I've coached many "successful" people who came to me because their lives had gone flat, and they had become uninspired and tepid. What happened? For many of them, they got comfortable. For years, they had pushed their comfort zones to get where they wanted to be. But as soon as they chose certainty over uncertainty, they stopped achieving. They hit the wall.

Why does it happen? Because when you've accomplished one of your goals, when you're rich and successful, the future naturally *seems* a little more certain. I'm sure we'd all feel a little more secure with a million bucks or so in the bank.

But that mindset shift is exactly what creates the environment for our ultimate undoing. When we're no longer uncertain about money, the desire—the need even—to pursue it recedes. When we're no longer uncertain about success, our ambition can blunt or mellow. We get to wallow in our bloated illusion of certainty. Eventually we get to do that thing called "settle." We settle for certainty.

That's the kind of power that uncertainty has in our lives. It can make us or break us. It can make us rich or make us poor. It can be the key to our success or drive us in the other direction.

For many people, it ends up being both.

## CHASING WHAT DOESN'T EXIST

The funny thing is, no matter how much you chase certainty, you'll never really be able to hold it or retain it. That's because it doesn't exist. The universe will always send us little reminders of its chaos and power, and no one is exempt from the prompting.

Nothing is certain. You could go to sleep tonight and never wake up. You could get in your car and never make it to work. Certainty is a complete illusion. Voodoo.

Some of you might find this terrible to think about, but it's true. No matter how hard we may try, we can never predict exactly what life will bring. Our plans will falter at some point eventually.

By running from uncertainty in search of certainty, we're actually rejecting the one thing in life that is guaranteed in favor of something that's nothing more than a fantasy.

"All I know," Socrates once said, "is that I know nothing." Many wise people understand this. In fact, they owe their wisdom to that very realization—that they don't actually know a damn thing.

Because when we think we know everything, we inadvertently turn ourselves away from the unknown and, by default, whole new realms of success. The person who accepts how unpredictable and uncertain life is has no choice but to embrace it.

They're not afraid of the uncertain; it's just a part of life. They don't seek out certainty because they know it doesn't really exist. They are also the kind of people who are aware of and open to the real magic and miracles of life and what can be accomplished.

One of the pillars of philosophy is the examination of how we know what we know. How can we prove that what we believe is true? In most cases, we can't.

In reality, even many of the things we think of as hard facts aren't. They're half-truths. They're assumptions. They're misinterpretations. They're guesses. They're based on cognitive biases, faulty information, or conditioning. Use science as an example. What we believed five, ten, or twenty years ago has since been disproved. We have made radical leaps in understanding and those leaps are continuing every day. What we know today will one day be looked upon as archaic and outdated.

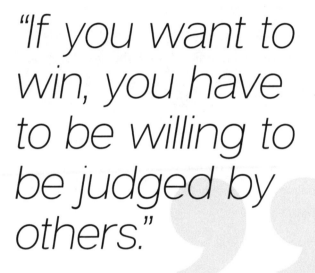

"If you want to win, you have to be willing to be judged by others."

Consider those same limits of understanding are everywhere in your life.

If we can't even be certain about what we "know" today, how can we know what will happen tomorrow?

As you've probably noticed, when you do try to stay in your comfort zone, you never truly feel comfortable. There's always that nagging feeling that you could be doing more. There's always that desire for a life that's better than the one you have now.

The more we try to stay comfortable today, the more uncomfortable we'll be tomorrow. There really is no destination, there is only exploring, exploring, and exploring.

## STEP FORWARD AND BE JUDGED

Like plenty of other things in our lives, part of our aversion to uncertainty comes from our fear of being judged by others. We are, in a very real way, afraid of what the tribe thinks and the prospect of being thrown out into the mystery and uncertainty of the wild.

If we put ourselves in uncomfortable situations, maybe we'll look awkward. People will think we're "weird." If we push our limits and try to achieve new things, maybe we'll fail. People will think we're a "failure."

> *"If you want to improve, be content to be thought foolish and stupid."*
> *- Epictetus*

You're never going to achieve your true potential if you're hooked by what other people think. In fact, you could change your life overnight if you simply abandoned the notion that other people's opinions matter. Life goes on, opinion-heavy or opinion-lite.

That doesn't mean you should go off and become a brazen sociopath and completely disregard what others think. But if you want to win, you have to be willing to be judged by others and not let it get to you. If you want to do something truly great, you'll have to accept that some people are going to think you're delusional or an idiot or self-righteous.

The person who avoids the uncertain doesn't do this. They're too afraid of being judged. They're too afraid to look foolish or stupid. They are stopped, one foot nailed to the floor by an illusion.

## EMBRACING THE UNCERTAIN

This can all come as quite a shock. Some of you are probably squirming in your chair as you read this.

That's because you're rejecting and avoiding uncertainty. You're afraid of it. You're trying to control and know things that you simply can't know or control. You're caught up in the la-la land that we are all born into and can never quite seem to get out of.

The good news is, it doesn't have to be that way.

That's why I want you to shift your thinking. Embrace the uncertainty. That's your personal assertion: ***"I embrace the uncertainty."***

Meet it head on. Cherish it. Enjoy it.

Remember, all of the successes, all of the experiences, all of the things you've always dreamed of are waiting for you in uncertainty. Once you accept this, it's not as scary as before. Sure, you might still be nervous about what will happen, but you'll also be hopeful and excited at the prospect of what may come.

While the unknown can hold plenty of bad things, it also holds everything good as well. It's overflowing with opportunity and progress.

I challenge you to go out today and take the bull by the horns and embrace your own uncertainty. Do the things you normally wouldn't. Shake up that daily routine. Dare to dream, dare to risk and startle your life into life.

Start with simple things. Take a different route to work. Instead of bringing your lunch or eating at the same few places, try somewhere you've never been. Start a conversation with the waiter or cashier. Smile and say hello to the people you pass on the street, or give them a friendly nod. Talk to that girl or guy who caught your eye.

Or maybe you're a natural extrovert who does all of that already. What are the things that make you uncomfortable? What are the things you'd like to do but avoid because of uncertainty?

Do them. Starting now. There's no better time than this moment. Develop and grow that muscle to be with the uncertain in life. To be with the glory of life itself, unconstrained by your own limits and opinions.

Don't stop there. Instead of simply stretching our comfort zone, let's blow the thing up completely. Try acting in a way you'd never think about acting. Doing something completely out of character would be a great start. Embrace that uncertainty and strike a blow for your future!

## OPPORTUNITY HUNTING

Embracing uncertainty has the power to transform your life, from your personal relationships to your career. It can help you get in shape, make more money, or find your future spouse.

You'll no longer be hiding from life, you'll be living it, drinking from it and enlivened by it.

When you stop searching for certainty, when you quit trying to make sense of everything, a lot of your stress will simply melt away. There really is nothing to figure out. If you took the time to be with what I'm saying, you'd realize that what causes most of your worry is trying to predict the future and then refusing to accept things when they don't or aren't going to go your way.

Life is an adventure. It's absolutely filled with opportunity. But it's up to you to embrace those opportunities fully and completely in all of their majestic, unnerving, and invigorating uncertainty.

Focus on the things you can control and release yourself from worrying about what you can't, like the weather, the Dow Jones, or what your neighbor thinks about your haircut.

"I embrace the uncertainty." This one simple statement can completely change the way you live, moment to moment to moment. The only thing that's guaranteed in life is that it's uncertain. The only thing we know is that we know nothing.

Go ahead, say it, embrace it: "I embrace the uncertainty."

# "I am not my thoughts; I am what I do."

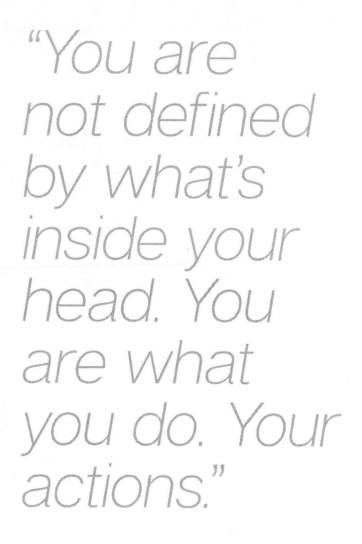

"You are
not defined
by what's
inside your
head. You
are what
you do. Your
actions."

# CHAPTER 6

# "Change your thoughts, change your life."

I was scrolling through Facebook recently when I came across this little gem. It had more likes than Justin Bieber and comments up the yin-yang.

As I sat there in my crimson smoking jacket and pale yellow cravat, I pondered its philosophical weight while sipping softly at the edges of my evening crème de menthe. (Okay, I was wearing an old AC/DC T-shirt and sweatpants and drinking coffee, but you get the picture). After a moment, I thought to myself, "What a complete pile of bullshit that is."

Imagine this: you're at work, you've got something to do, but you're dreading it, just not "feeling it" today. You glance at the clock. 10:34. Ah well, at least it's not long until lunch.

"Hmm, what will I eat today? Oh, I've been wanting to try that new place down the street. My coworker said it's really good. But I really should stick to my budget..."

You suddenly snap back to reality and find yourself staring at the blinking cursor on your computer screen.

"Wow, I suck at this. I'm just not up for it today. I need some energy."

Before you know it, you've opened your browser and are scrolling through one of your favorite time-wasting sites.

"Wowzer! Hover-shoes?! I could really use some of those!!"

Quick step back to reality. You check your e-mail. A message from your credit card company. "I'm in so much debt. I'm never going to get out of this mess. No hover-shoes or lunch out for me."

A notification from that online dating site you signed up for a few weeks ago. "I'll never find someone. My love life is a disaster. Maybe relationships and I just don't match."

Someone walks past your cubicle. You frantically click your mouse and mash on the keyboard, feigning busyness for the unsuspecting intruder. "Whew, that was close!"

Look at the clock again. 11:13. Another half an hour wasted. "I should really get to work . . . right after I . . ."

Is any of this sounding familiar? Maybe you don't work in an office, but you can still relate to that feeling of dread that hits when you're faced with something you've been resisting. Like you'd rather do anything than the task at hand. That "to-do" list quickly becomes a "don't-wanna-do" list.

Even if you're married or already in a relationship you might also identify with those feelings of undesirability. When your thoughts about your situation have become more consuming and debilitating than everything else. When you have become so distracted from what your relationship is supposed to be about, so embroiled in the should/shouldn'ts, could/couldn'ts, and who's right or wrong you often wonder why the hell you're still in it at all.

The truth is, we all do this from time to time. Even the most driven, most successful, and wisest among us have these kinds of thoughts.

So what is it that separates those successful people from you and me? They understand (consciously or otherwise) one simple thing: what they think and what they do don't always have to align.

## YOU ARE NOT YOUR THOUGHTS

You are not your thoughts. You are not defined by what's inside your head. You are what you do. Your actions.

> *"Great thoughts speak only to the thoughtful mind, but great actions speak to all mankind."*
>
> *– Theodore Roosevelt*

Most of us let our internal condition weigh heavily on what we do. But the truly great performers are great precisely because they've learned to experience those feelings while sidestepping the inclination to act upon them.

It's not that they never doubt themselves or never have a desire to procrastinate or avoid a particular situation. It's not that they always "feel" like doing what they should.

They simply focus and lean in. They act anyway.

It'd be great if we could simply decide to never have a negative thought, but when it comes down to it, that's just not realistic. I know, I know, my positive-thinking peeps are losing their minds at this statement but here's something for even those people to consider. Haven't you wondered why you came up with positivity as an answer to your life in the first place? Have you ever noticed how you are when impacted or surrounded by apparently negative people or situations? That's right, even you get gripped by the old negative hand now and again no matter how you might try and avoid it.

The truth is, it's difficult to have a say in, let alone control, what you think about. Especially because, as we've established elsewhere in this book, we're not even aware of the majority of things we think about.

We have just as many pointless, irrelevant thoughts as important ones. Then there are those default thoughts that pop into your head day in and day out. Thoughts of unworthiness, being judged, not belonging, or some lack of competence. All of this while going to work, paying your bills, going to the grocery store, or driving your car!

Many of the things I teach my clients involve changing the way you approach and look at life. But these are long-term solutions. Ultimately my goal is to help you shift your subconscious. And that, my dears, is like turning a battleship. It takes time.

No matter how hard you try, you're going to have the occasional negative thought. Maybe more than occasionally. Maybe every day. Maybe hundreds of times per day.

You're going to have days when you don't want to get out of bed, when you don't want to go to work, when you don't want to take care of your responsibilities. But you do. Every day you engage in activities that you don't *really* want to do. That means you already have a

*"You don't have to feel like today is your day; you just have to act like it is."*

muscle for having thoughts and acting independently of them.

As I consistently say to my clients, you don't have to feel like today is your day; you just have to act like it is.

Sure, it never hurts to be in the right kind of mood or mindset, but if we sit around waiting to be in the perfect mood, we're just never going to get started. I've come across literally thousands of people in my career who have spent their lives waiting to feel or think differently. And while inspiration or motivation may strike once in a while, they are fickle friends and can't be depended on to show up whenever you need them.

> *"We become just by performing just actions, temperate by performing temperate actions, brave by performing brave actions."*
> *– Aristotle*

You change your life by doing, not by thinking about doing. In fact, when you become closely associated with the actions you are taking, something magical starts to become apparent.

Thoughts without actions are just that, thoughts, and your negative thoughts about yourself, others, or your circumstances will have no impact on your success as long as you leave them where they lie.

## HOW DOING CHANGES YOUR THINKING

The benefits of doing are twofold.

Doing gets you doing what you need to do, of course. But it is, ironically, also the quickest way to change your thoughts.

There are a couple reasons for this. We know your thoughts can become your reality. And when your reality is one of acting on the things that are in your best interests, your thoughts will actually shift to match that. Think about this: your thoughts (and the resulting feelings) are not always aligned with what is in the best interests of your life, your health, your finances, or your potential. Many times those same thoughts and feelings are pulling you away from your potential. Things like doubt, fear, procrastination, or frustration rule the day instead of the kind of positive action that will actually forward your life.

If you always attack the task at hand without hesitation, what will you think the next time you have something important to do? Your thoughts start to become intuitive action over time until you start to act independently of your negative thoughts time after time after time. Are you going to think about yourself and what you lack, or are you going to deal with the actions presenting themselves right there in that moment of time?

Haven't you ever noticed, when you're fully immersed in something, all of your problems or negative conversations seem to disappear? When you are cognitively and genuinely engaged in a practice or project, that internal chatter gets quieter and quieter. The golfers, tennis players, meditators, knitters, musicians, artists, and runners among us know exactly what I am talking about. Athletes call this "the zone." And the good news is, you can get better at getting in the zone, too!

When you can focus your attention on the action at hand, eventually your consciousness starts to get the idea.

Each time you do, you build your experience of self-confidence and trust in yourself. All of that impacts the long-term way in which you think.

So what's the second way that actions influence our thoughts?

Remember when I said your thoughts can become your reality? That's true. While your thoughts can become your reality, it's *only* through your actions that your thoughts actually *become your life.* Until then, they are only thoughts.

Sometimes our mind is like the equivalent of a fun-house mirror, distorting and contorting and blurring our lives and our potential.

Our minds often have an unrealistic perception of the world, peppered with interpretation, misunderstanding, automatic behaviors and opinions, and cultural and familial programming all laid on top of our lives like designs on a giant sheet of tracing paper; the more we strive to get our reality to match this design, the more we struggle.

The gap between how life *is* and how we *think* life is, is often the black hole in which we fruitlessly labor.

We think things are worse or better, harder or easier than they actually are due to this cacophony of background noise and judgement.

Consider this: you just messed up something important. Immediately thoughts like "I'm so stupid" and "I always screw things up" randomly pop into your head.

All this means is that your reaction to one situation is out of sync with the whole. Just like when you whine (yes, you whine) about how "impossible" what you need to do is. Your brain starts to follow that line of thought all the way down the rabbit hole!

Fortunately, by accepting and including your thoughts as just a small part of the whole and getting down to taking actions, you'll slowly start to realize just how out of touch you've been all along.

This method is actually similar to one used by psychiatrists giving therapy to their patients. That's because it works. By challenging our thoughts with actions and exposing ourselves to the situations we resist, we train our brain to see the world more cognitively. We get accustomed to living life "as is" rather than how we think it is!

The next time you're feeling or experiencing any sort of negative or diminishing thought that disempowers you, move on immediately. Act independently of that thought. More specifically, act in a way that's in your best interests rather than in a way that is dominated by how you automatically think and feel. Each time will be better than the last until your mind wakes up and realizes, "Hey, I can do this. I'm learning!"

## ACTION GREASES THE WHEEL OF LIFE

*"Inaction breeds doubt and fear. Action breeds confidence and courage. If you want to conquer fear, do not sit home and think about it. Go out and get busy."*
– Dale Carnegie

I like what Dale says here. When we choose action instead of inaction, when we act beyond our automatic thoughts, something interesting happens: we start to forget about the things that are bothering us.

Simply put, when we act, we just don't have time for anything else! It's hard to focus on your internal worrying and nay-saying when you're busy getting things done. It's all about momentum. Once you've started rolling, it's easier to stay moving. That road that looked so long and intimidating before starts to blur as you speed across it.

But you've got to put your key in the ignition, crank 'er up, and put it in drive first. The car isn't going to start itself and then wait patiently for you in the driveway.

When you think about it, that's basically what most of us do. We want to be driven. We think a more productive mood will chauffeur us through life, a confident mood will make things easier or more doable. But if you want to get to where you're going, you'll have to take the wheel.

You have to buckle in and stomp hard on that gas pedal, whether you're ready to or not.

Today, I want you to do something different than what you normally do. I want you to act in a way that's independent of your typical negative or unproductive thoughts. Act on the moment and in line with what the item in front of your face demands of you. Fuck how you feel, ACT!

Don't wait for the mood to strike. Don't get stuck looking for that magic feeling that will do the work for you.

Simply act. Put aside your thoughts and move.

It's not about psyching yourself up. It's not about getting everything aligned just right. Just act. Do it.

Not in a minute. Not after this show is over. Now.

Of course, your mind will always try to rationalize *not* acting. It'll remind you of all the other things you could be doing. It'll drudge up all your recent stresses and doubts.

But don't act on your thoughts. Act on what's in front of you.

Change your life by changing your actions. That's the only way.

Still need more motivation? Think about the greatest people you know of—either personally or by reputation. Do you consider their thoughts? Or do you remember their actions?

Do you think Gandhi or Rosa Parks or Abraham Lincoln were never gripped by thoughts of doubt, fear, or uncertainty? How about Nikola Tesla or Steve Jobs? Do you seriously think those people woke up every day in the perfect mood with "Everything's Coming Up Roses" playing in their heads? HELL NO! They were racked by the same kind of shit you are, but they acted ANYWAY. They rolled up whatever was in their way, set it aside, and strode out into the unknown. It wasn't a passive endeavor. Their greatness didn't just miraculously float out into the ether for us to consume. If they hadn't taken action, we'd have never known what their passions were in the first place. We'd never have witnessed their greatness or wisdom.

They toiled, doubted, and had sleepless nights; they worried and battled and ground it out until their lives and their work finally aligned.

I mean, come on, chances are you can think of plenty of people, past and present, who appeared to have "good thoughts" but never accomplished much.

That's what we become when we're more worried about how we think than what we do.

On the other hand, think of how many people with negative thoughts have gone on to become wildly successful.

All the legendary musicians with drug problems. All the pro athletes with anger management issues. The models with unhealthy body images. The millionaires with scarcity mindsets.

We could go on and on. The point is, positive thinking isn't a predictor of accomplishment any more than negative thinking indicates failure. All of the people described above acted independently of their internal condition. You can, too.

It's all about action. Going out there, doing it, and taking all your negative bullshit along for the ride. It's never going to get any better, any easier, or any more understandable. This is it, life is now and you're never going to have a better moment than this.

Don't know what to do or where to start? Good, that's your first action. Find out, understand. Trawl the internet, read books, ask questions, take courses, seek advice, do whatever you need to do to unfuck yourself and get into your life.

Get up on your feet and get going.

> *"Action may not bring happiness, but there is no happiness without action."*
> *- Benjamin Disraeli*

## SEPARATING YOUR THOUGHTS FROM WHO YOU ARE

### *"I am not my thoughts; I am what I do."*

That's your newest personal assertion, the phrase that sums it all up. Go ahead, try it out. "I am not my thoughts; I am what I do."

You are not your thoughts. They're just a bunch of random things running through your head. Many of them you have no control over.

Eventually we'd all like to have better, more positive thoughts. But sitting there isn't going to make it happen.

It's when we challenge our bodies and minds, when we experience, when we face our fears, when we accomplish—even when we fail—that we truly change who we are.

You could be the smartest person in the world, but that doesn't mean a thing if you don't take action.

Remember that the next time you're not "feeling it." When you're not in the mood to go to work or take a significant step in life. When you're doubting yourself too much to get started.

Forget all of it. Just take that first step. And the next one. And the next one.

You are not your thoughts. Act. You are what you do.

# "I am relentless."

"Our biggest successes are born out of discomfort, uncertainty, and risk."

# CHAPTER 7

# Think back to some of your biggest successes in life.

Maybe you made a really big sale, started a new business, or bought a house. Maybe you got married to the love of your life or went back to school or completed a marathon. It could be anything you're truly proud of.

How the hell did you achieve it?

Well, you probably weren't sitting on the couch pondering your navel. Chances are you weren't wrapped up in the humdrum of your everyday existence, either, or mentally calculating the sharp rise in the price of milk since 1977.

So what was it?

I may not be able to guess exactly what you were doing, but I can be certain of one thing: you were uncomfortable. Put a slightly different way, you were most likely operating outside of your "comfort zone."

From the nervousness and doubt we feel when we take risks in our careers, to the muscle soreness and shortness of breath we experience pumping out another five minutes on the treadmill, our biggest successes are born out of discomfort, uncertainty, and risk.

> *"Nothing in the world is worth having or worth doing unless it means effort, pain, difficulty."*
> *- Theodore Roosevelt*

In fact, the greater the degree of discomfort you experience, the greater the difficulty, the greater the sense of personal accomplishment that comes after.

And that's exactly why great accomplishments and extraordinary successes are so rare. Because most people don't like being uncomfortable.

## BEING RELENTLESS

Anytime you're working to achieve something, you're going against the current. Often the opinions of the people around you are trying to push and pull you away from your destination.

They'll say you can't do it, you're making a mistake, it's impossible, you'll fail. The more unique and out-of-the-box your endeavor is, the stronger the pushback can be. Why? Well, mostly because the other people in your life have gotten used to relating to you as a specific "kind" of person. So anytime you attempt to break out of that mold, you're not only messing with your own world, you're also messing with theirs.

And the resistance doesn't just come from other people; it comes from your own mind, too. Both your conscious and subconscious thoughts can work against you to stop your dreams right in their tracks.

It could be outright negative—"That's impossible. Why even try?" Or it could be subtler.

"Wouldn't it be a lot better to just sleep in instead of getting an early jump on things at the office?"

"That game on your phone is so much more fun than working."

You could overcome these distractions and objections, of course, as we discussed in the last chapter. But there comes a point on your journey when you sometimes lose track of where you are. You become so locked up in the daily humdrum that you've completely wandered off the path and into the middle of the fucking jungle, and are now meandering around with no map, no water, and no clue.

Are you going in the right direction? How long until you get there? How much more of this can you take? Maybe it's over here. No wait, maybe it's this way.

And when you inevitably stumble or encounter some sort of obstacle, you question the journey at all. Maybe it's even time to turn back.

At this point, when you don't know whether you're up or down, how far you have to go or how far you've come, there's only one thing that can keep you going.

That thing is relentlessness. The momentum to keep moving and moving and moving, no matter what happens.

It doesn't matter if we're "feeling it," it doesn't matter if we're gripped by doubt and worry.

Here's the deal: true relentlessness comes when the only thing you have left is relentlessness. When it seems all is lost and all hope and evidence for success have long since vanished, relentlessness is the fuel that drives you through.

## IT'S ONLY TRUE IF YOU AGREE

The most successful among us got to where they are today because they transcended obstacles.

But that's easier said than done. It's one thing to say "never give up" (I fucking hate bumper-sticker slogans), but quite another to actually put relentlessness into your life's most worthy causes.

Listen, when it comes down to it, the world doesn't stop you from succeeding; you're not that big of a deal. The universe is conspiring neither for nor against you, and the only thing that stops you is when you buy into the notion that you are stopped. Then, my friend, you really *are* stopped. Until then, it's on like freaking Donkey Kong.

*"It is the mark of an educated mind to be able to entertain a thought without accepting it."*

*– Aristotle*

Think about all of the things that have been accomplished in human history that were once considered "impossible." If you told someone from the 1850s that you could fly from California to China in a hollow metal tube filled with hundreds of people, they'd have more than likely sent you to the local insane asylum for the rest of your days.

But the Wright brothers didn't accept that flight was impossible. They simply didn't accept that thought—even though there was no historical evidence to prove that human flight *was* possible.

Even though they had no physical proof and it had never been done before, they were determined to make it happen and they were relentless in its pursuit.

Now compare that to your own problems. If you're like most people, your goals probably aren't nearly as ambitious as inventing the first airplane.

You probably just want to make more money, face your fears, find your soul mate, lose some weight,

"Sometimes you just have to grind it out, stake your claim, and hustle for what you want."

or strike a blow for a better life—things that have been done millions of times before, and will be done again and again in the future, by people just as capable as you.

These goals ARE possible. However, don't be fooled by the self-help bullshit that tells you "You deserve it!" Because you don't. No one does. That conversation will leave you waiting and wanting and eventually a complete victim to your own life. Sometimes you just have to grind it out, stake your claim, and hustle for what you want. You will need to quite literally **make** it happen.

So when someone looks at you and says, "You'll never make a million dollars," or your brain is telling you, "It's impossible for you to lose one hundred pounds," you have two choices. You can succumb to the notion that you don't know what you're doing, that you lack the resources, that you don't have what it takes, or that you or your life needs to be fixed before you can do those things. And then you can quit.

Or you can disagree. You can absolutely refuse to accept it and reach for your greatness. You can say, "No, you're wrong, and I'm going to prove it."

The impossible only becomes possible in the moment you believe it is.

> *"We would accomplish more things if we did not think of them as impossible."*
> – Vince Lombardi

Here's the crazy thing: you can never really prove what's possible or impossible.

You could throw yourself at something a thousand times, failing miserably on every attempt, and yet succeed on attempt #1,001.

The truth is, you can never really know. We never really have all the facts. As humans, we still only understand a tiny fraction of our own minds, let alone the world or the oceans or space or technology. If someone tells you they have all the answers, call them out on that bullshit. The truth is they're winging it just like you, just like everyone else. Answers? Gimme a freaking break!

So if we can't even say for certain that it's impossible to put a man on Mars, how can any of us know what we're really capable of in the day-to-day living of our lives?

They can't. The only question is whether you agree with what you can and cannot do. An opinion only becomes true when you accept it and stop acting on your potential.

My own life is an example of what's possible when you live life beyond your own beliefs and the views of others. I was a pretty average high-school student, but I've gone on to travel the world and coach thousands and thousands of people. I've guided doctors, lawyers, politicians, actors, celebrities, athletes, CEOs—hell, I've even coached Catholic priests in Ireland and Buddhist monks in Thailand!

There's a wondrous, magical life out there waiting for you in the unknown and, while it's not all cherry pies and bubble gum, there is a reality that you can accomplish that's far beyond the one you're currently wasting away in.

## BLAZING THE RELENTLESS TRAIL

To see this idea of relentlessness in action, let's look at a major success story that you and I are likely to be familiar with: Arnold Schwarzenegger.

Arnold was born to relatively poor parents in a small town in Austria, just a couple of years after the end of World War II.

Yet young Arnold dreamt of going to America and acting in movies. What do you think his parents thought of that dream? What do you think his fellow Austrian townsfolk told him about his ambitions or whispered behind his back?

Remember, we're not talking about today, where we have television and Internet and smartphones and anyone with a wireless connection can become a celebrity. Back then, most households didn't even have a TV.

"America" was a nebulous, fantastical concept for Arnold and the people he grew up with—a place they had only seen in pictures or movies.

So you can pretty much guarantee that everyone he knew thought there was no chance he'd ever realize his dream, and if he had accepted that at any point, their words would have come true.

If he had agreed that he wouldn't become a world famous bodybuilder, it would've been true. If he had agreed that he couldn't move to America, he wouldn't have. If he had accepted that he'd never make it into movies or he'd never be a star actor or he couldn't become governor, he would have quit.

But he never agreed with what the world or other people told him about what was and wasn't possible.

He was relentless. He spent hours in the gym every day, pushing his body. He practiced his bodybuilding poses. He read books. He learned business. He auditioned for movie roles.

Relentlessly. Giving up or changing plans simply wasn't an option.

And if you look at his path, you can learn something valuable about relentlessness: sometimes, it's all you have.

Before Arnold, no Austrian bodybuilder had ever gone on to become an A-list action star in the United States, let alone be elected governor of California. You can be sure he spent a good part of his life and career not really knowing where he was going. There aren't any road signs when you're trekking through uncharted territory; it's all discovery and exploration. You are blazing a trail, not following one.

When you find yourself in that situation, all you can do is focus on and deal with what's directly in front of you.

You just put one foot in front of the other, taking things on as they present themselves.

Even Arnold, who had a big, grand vision, ultimately achieved it by taking one step at a time.

He'd go to the gym and start working his biceps. He'd focus on each movement, each rise and fall of the dumbbell, rep after rep after rep, feeling his muscles flex and tear and grow.

Then when he was done with biceps, he'd move on to shoulders. And then back. And then glutes. And then quads. And then calves.

As he worked each respective muscle group, he gave it his full attention. And then it was on to the next one, moment by moment by moment.

When he had worked each muscle, each body part, to exhaustion, he went home. But there he was the next day, doing it all over again. Relentlessly.

Look more recently at people like Malala Yousafzai, who stands for the rights of women and children in Afghanistan; or Michael Phelps and his record-breaking athletic accomplishments; or Jessica Cox, born without arms and currently flying commercial airlines.

Are you getting the picture here?

The key to becoming relentless is to focus on the problem in front of you. Give it your full attention. Become someone who progresses even when all seems lost. The answer is always out there; all you need to do is find it.

Then you can move forward to your next obstacle. And you give that obstacle your full attention until it's taken care of. Then there's the next and the next and the next.

By doing this, you never have to wonder where you're going. You're not worried about how many miles you have left to walk. You become someone who loves obstacles rather than avoids them because obstacles are your keys to success and growth. You simply take one step at a time.

And if you come upon something that's blocking your path, you find a way to get over it or get around it. Then you keep walking.

Relentlessness doesn't mean charging into the fray headfirst, swinging and flailing your arms every which way. It's focused, determined action. Again and again and again.

You're not bashing your fist against a brick wall until it's bloody and bruised. You're using your hammer and chisel to slowly, methodically chip away piece by piece until eventually there's a hole.

And then the hole gets bigger. And bigger. And before you know it, you're like Alice stepping through the looking glass to a whole new world.

## YOU ARE RELENTLESS

When you're not sure if you're following the right path, when you've been knocked down a few too many times, it's completely fine to get discouraged, hell, even defeated. What's not okay is to stop.

Because you can always lean on relentlessness. When you have nothing else, you have relentlessness.

Rather than worrying about whether you should keep going or turn back, press in relentlessly. Relentlessness has one direction, and that's forward. It only has one option, and that's to keep the momentum going.

There is no giving up. There is no quitting. There is no changing of plans.

Relentless is the bodybuilder who goes to the gym for hours every day. Relentless is the prospective entrepreneur who has been ridiculed or rejected for their completely original idea but keeps pitching it anyway. Relentless is the overweight mom who feels like she's never going to get there. Relentless is the newly minted college graduate at the bottom of the corporate ladder barely making enough to pay her rent and yet staying at the office later than anyone else just to learn as much as she can. Relentless is you.

Anyone who's ever gone to the gym knows that the results aren't immediate. You don't spend thirty minutes on the treadmill and look like a new person.

But that doesn't mean what you're doing isn't working. You're making progress. With each exercise, each step, each movement, each action, you get a little better, a little closer.

Until one day you look in the mirror and think, "Wow!"

It's the same thing with your business or your health, or your career or your relationships. Even when you don't see anything happening, it is. Even when you're not quite hitting the mark, you're making progress.

Until one day you look at your bank balance or your new job or your children or your new house and think, "Wow!"

That's why you have to keep going. Relentlessly.

Because when you're trekking through the jungle, you don't know if you're three days from civilization or thirty minutes. All you can do is walk. The only way out is forward.

Sit up, straighten your spine, and repeat after me: "I am relentless."

# "I expect nothing and accept everything."

"Stop doing all that shit you know you shouldn't be doing and start doing all the shit you know you should be doing."

# CHAPTER 8

Firstly, do not be deceived by the title of this chapter. There is something truly amazing for you to discover in the following pages.

Imagine this.

You've always dreamed of starting your own business—being your own boss, controlling your own schedule, and really building something you can be proud of, something you can point to as a major life accomplishment.

Through a combination of hard work, determination, and solid planning, you've managed to organize your life in such a way that this dream of yours can now become a reality.

You've already come up with a great business idea, hired a company to create a cool logo and branding, and now it's time to get to work. Here's where the fun begins . . .

You'll need a store, of course. And that's the first task you tackle, spending the next week driving around town, scouting locations and negotiating with real estate agents.

It's not easy, but you finally find what you think is a pretty good location, for a pretty good price. There was another place you really had your eye on, but you couldn't make it work within the budget.

There are a few other things to get taken care of, like property insurance, a business license, and setting up your taxes. Even though you've yet to make a dollar, you've already had to hire an accountant to help you sort through those complicated business taxes.

Oh well, on to the next project. Your store will need furniture and other necessary equipment, so you shop around to get a rate on that. Another thing off the checklist.

Obviously you'll need someone to work there, too. Time to hire some employees. Check.

It's all going pretty well until . . . BOOM! That deal you had fought for and ground out to secure the unique product you were planning to sell fell through and now you have to look for alternatives. SHIT! Your heart sinks and breathing shallows as you frantically search out wholesalers, importers, manufacturers—anyone who can help—and start asking for quotes.

The only problem is, the new prices you're being quoted are way beyond your pricing model. How can you make this thing work? You tirelessly continue searching but keep coming up zero after zero after zero. This is fast becoming a disaster!

You've already invested massive amounts of time and resources into this and now you've hit a big fat roadblock. You're realizing now that you should have seen this coming. This is business; stuff is bound to go wrong. The cascading stream of doubt and second-guessing washes through your brain with a heavy rinse cycle of reality.

"Dammit this was going too smoothly; I just **knew** something like this would happen!!"

This feeling builds and grows until it starts to pull you under. Setting up a business means risking everything you've ever worked for. Is it even worth it? You've got bills, for the love of God!

Now that you **really** think about it, you've spent more time working on this project than you did at your last job. A LOT more. I mean come on, it's been day and night with hardly a breath. You have less control of your time than you ever did before. Your every thought, second, and dollar has been geared toward this thing. Why did you ever think it was better to work for yourself?

This isn't what you signed up for, is it? Maybe this whole thing was a mistake. You're starting to feel a little darker and more depressed while you start to confront the gut-churning possibility that you might lose all that investment and wind up having to crawl back to your old boss to ask if you can return to your old job.

WHOOOAAAAA!!!!!

Easy, tiger! Before we get ahead of ourselves, let's take a step back.

## EXPECTING THE EXPECTED

What's really going on here?

It's simple. You, like everybody else, are weighed down by expectation.

I'm not talking about the usual kind of everyday expectations you're aware of. It's also not like we're literally saying to ourselves, "I expect this," or, "I expected that," in a conscious way. It's something that's happening just below the surface, where you'll only see it if you take the time to look closely.

No, I'm talking about the ugly, undermining, hidden, and treacherous expectations that dwell in the wings and under the stage of your Broadway blockbuster. The kind of expectations you didn't even know you had until they came out of nowhere and blindsided you and sucked the air from your lungs.

When you and I take on a life-changing project, we prepare for it from what we know. That includes items from our own experience, what we've read, heard, and imagined. We start to picture it in our minds. We research, we ask others for their opinions, and consume reams of information. We begin to assemble an idea of what this will look like and how we're going to get there. That image in our heads becomes the template from which we work and plan.

What we **don't** see is that we're also setting up a world of hidden expectations—the cracks and crevices hidden in the foundation of our best-laid plans that can kill off a potential idea before it really gets going. In our business example, our budding entrepreneur "didn't expect" to lose his deal for product and while losing that deal was bad enough, the interruption to his expectation was actually the biggest blow to his aspirations.

How do you know if you have hidden expectations in your life? If you have places in your life where you experience disappointment, resentment, regret, suppression, anger, lethargy, essentially anywhere you are deflated or have some loss of your personal chutzpah or any other suppressive emotion, you have these expectations. Any place where you're just not *yourself*—if you look at these places long enough, you'll see the reality of that area of your life is in some way short of the scenario you had anticipated in your mind's eye. If you are upset in your marriage, you'll see a gap between your expectations of how it was "supposed" to be and how it in fact is. For others it might be your finances, your weight loss, new job, etc.

Your powerlessness is directly correlated to the gap between your hidden expectations and your reality. The greater the gap, the worse you'll actually feel.

I read somewhere that the root cause of upset in marriage is **unmet** expectation.

I think it goes out further, much further. I say the problem is expectation itself. I contend that the upsets strewn throughout your entire life are a product of thousands of unspoken or unrecognized expectations that cast a giant shadow across your life experience, causing great stress when you're trying to make life fit with your expectations and great disappointment when life doesn't match up to them.

Here's what else they do: they actually get in the way of our **real** lives, our real issues and items that require attention. They are like a mirage that diverts us from our genuine power and clouds our ability to take pronounced, decisive action. In short, you end up working on your expectations and having life line up with **them** rather than taking the actions that would positively impact your situation. This "sidetracking" draws your power away from what's actually going to improve your life or accomplish your goal, down a pathway of no power, no results, and wasted time.

## CUTTING OUT THE MIDDLE MAN OF EXPECTATION

Now that we've busted our problems with expectations wide open, you'll start to realize something. And that's that many of the difficulties and complications in your life are the direct result of expectations that you have or have had.

We've been using an example of a business plan gone wrong, but, in your own life, your failed relationships, dissatisfaction with work, and abandoned diets can be traced right back to expectation. How many times have you said to yourself, "This isn't how I thought it would be"?

What about the last time you were angry with someone? Can you remember it?

Take a moment to examine that situation, and you'll soon realize that your anger was a product of expectations. The gap between how it is and how it should have been. You harbor an unspoken expectation that people in your life will be agreeable, you expect them to tell the truth and follow through on any agreements you have with them. Expect, expect, expect. And when they don't match those expectations? Oh boy!

"This is all great and good, Mr. Scottish-man, but how in the hell do I uncover *my* hidden expectations?"

Easy. Pick an area of your life in which things aren't going as well as you'd like them to, maybe even somewhere in your life that sucks right now. Take a pen and piece of paper and write out how that area was "supposed" to turn out. How had you planned it?

How should this have gone? You might have to use your imagination and sense of wonder to get in touch with how the future looked from back there. Get in touch with the hope and positivity of that area and where it was supposed to head. Describe it in as much detail as you can possibly recall.

Next, on a separate piece of paper, write down how this area *actually* looks. Again, make this an exhaustive description, not just "it sucks." Get into detail about why it is the way it is and what you now have to deal with. How do you feel now that this part of your life did not meet your expectations?

Now, look at both pieces of paper side by side. Your pain, anguish, disappointment (or whatever your thing is) is greater in the areas where the gap is widest between what you expected and what you actually have. In there are your hidden expectations. Do the work here until you fully uncover the expectations you had inadvertently set yourself up for.

Good, now look again. In what way does how you feel about this make a difference to your reality? Does it make it any better? Does it solve your issue? Hell no, it makes no positive difference whatso-freakin-ever! It even makes it WORSE!

Your problems don't derail you, your hidden expectations do!

The point here is that the "expectation" of how life should be doesn't do you any good. You're actually more winded by the whack your expectations took than the situation itself and that's the deal with expectations; they blow things out of proportion and dilute your power to deal with issues effectively and powerfully. Listen, it's not like I'm saying something radically new here; the notion of "letting go" of expectations has been around for thousands of years although, in our culture (that of the West), it's a practice very few engage in.

Here's the coaching—CUT IT OUT! Let go of those expectations NOW!

It's much more powerful to come to terms with life's unpredictability and to engage with your circumstances for what they actually are than get bogged down by your refusal to let go of unnecessary or unproductive expectations.

The world revolves around change. Birth and death, growth and destruction, rise and fall, summer and winter. It's never the same from one day to another no matter how much it might seem that it is.

> *"No man ever steps in the same river twice…"*
> *– Heraclitus*

Our minds would love to predict and plan for everything that's going to happen. But it's simply not possible. And these expectations not only have a negative effect on our emotional state, they actually leave us less powerful than we really could be.

It's so much more effective to simply take things as they present themselves, to live in the moment (like there's another moment you could live in), and solve issues and items as they arise, than to constantly expect.

It's not that I'm anti-planning (I most certainly am not), but the stone-cold attachment to the plan (and all the expectation therein) is a little like falling out of a rowboat and continuing to row even though you have no oars and no boat under you anymore. Your plan (and image) of how this should have gone is no longer relevant but you still struggle to reconcile the space between your expectations and reality.

Life can be like that at times. On some occasions you have to realize that the game has changed (sometimes dramatically so) and you need to pivot. Deal with your reality.

Wake up, you're in the water. Stop waving your arms about and paddle to shore, dammit!

## LIFE IS MORE OF A DANCE THAN A MARCH

Our mind has all kinds of automatic thought processes that we don't even know are going on. Expectations are just one of them, albeit an important one.

Here's the harsh truth about how our brain works.

We all like to believe in something called "free will." It's one of those concepts that really speaks to who we are as human beings. I mean, let's be honest, if we don't have free will, what in the hell do we have?

We value the notion that we freely choose what we do, and when to do it. We want to feel that we control our own fate and shape our own destiny.

But when our minds are ruled by these automatic thought processes, do we really have free will? Many would argue that we don't. Listen, here's how much free will you have—stop doing all that shit you know you shouldn't be doing and start doing all the shit you know you should be doing. All of it.

This free will stuff isn't so easy now, is it!?

> *"No man is free who is not master of himself."*
> *- Epictetus*

Because, as we've talked about throughout this book, even when you feel yourself making a conscious decision, there are a series of unconscious thought processes that are driving that choice. Things you don't even see or acknowledge.

People are much more irrational and illogical than we realize. In many cases, our subconscious is the puppet master that truly pulls the strings.

Fortunately, you can take back your freedom to choose. And that's by understanding how your mind works, seeing what it's doing as it does it, and being able to use that information to cognitively choose something else. To make conscious that which is currently unconscious.

Expectations are just one of these things.

## WHEN LIFE IS APPROPRIATE

**"I expect nothing and accept everything."** This is your final personal assertion.

Let me get clear about this one. This is not some meek, weak submission to life. No, this is the statement of a masterful celebrant of success, someone who cannot be dominated by anyone or anything.

When you expect nothing, you're living in the moment. You're not worrying about the future or rejecting the past. You're simply embracing your situation as it comes. When you accept everything, that doesn't mean you are okay with it or that you agree with it, but simply that you are owning it and in charge of it. Remember you can always change something when you can take ownership and responsibility for it. Sometimes it's the single most effective way of resolving your "stuff." Own it!

> *"Don't seek to have events happen as you wish, but wish them to happen as they do happen, and all will be well with you."*
> *- Epictetus*

The next time you catch yourself getting brought down by your expectations, shift things in a different direction. Instead of getting your knickers in a twist about how things didn't turn out the way you wanted or expected them to, simply accept them for what they are. In that moment you are now freed up to deal with them.

"This is appropriate." When you're having growing pains at your new job, take a step back and realize how appropriate that really is. Of course a new job is going to take some getting used to, whether it's the tasks you're performing or the people you work with. It's therefore entirely appropriate to make a few mistakes or tread carefully as you try to get to know your new colleagues. The expectations dissolve right there, immediately.

If your relationship is struggling, change your perspective and get the whole picture. What are your expectations?

Many of us expect our partners to be a certain way consistently, or to anticipate our needs and know exactly what we're feeling, as if by magic. But your partner, like you, is an imperfect human with his or her own set of complicated emotions and thoughts. So it's appropriate that they may sometimes be distracted or get short with you after a bad day.

We often expect other people to treat us exactly as we treat them. If we do them a favor, we expect to get the same favor back in return. It becomes an unspoken "debt" of sorts. When we give our partner a foot massage, we expect them to reciprocate either directly or indirectly. Those expectations grow in both weight and complexity in an intimate or romantic relationship.

You won't believe how much your interactions with other people will improve the moment you let go of expecting, the instant you learn to accept things as they happen.

Again, this doesn't mean you need to put up with shitty or abusive relationships. But the only thing more unpredictable than one person is two unpredictable people. If you are in one of those kinds of relationships, it's time for you to invoke the boat analogy. Stop rowing, the game has changed, shift your plan. Your partners, friends, and family members all have their own desires, perceptions, and feelings. While you're thinking one thing, they're more than likely thinking something completely different. That thing that's got you feeling pissed may not have even registered on their radar. They could be completely oblivious to what's going on with you.

Instead of silently expecting something and feeling slighted when it doesn't happen, let go of that expectation. If there's something you want, how about asking for it with no expectation? And when you do something positive or generous, do it because you genuinely want to rather than loading in the added weight of what you expect in return.

That game of tit for tat only hurts you both in the long run.

If it's something serious that consistently challenges the relationship, confront the other party about it. Don't expect them to realize how you feel or, by the same token, expect them to be able to change how you feel. They can't. Only you can do that.

People are always going to lie, steal, cheat, and everything else one can imagine. It's just not connected to reality to live in the expectation that they somehow won't and then throw a hissy fit when they do it anyway. Remember, in those cases, you always end up worse off than they do! Much worse!

You end up sticking yourself with resentment, regret, anger, or frustration. Remember, they're not doing that to you, you're doing that part to yourself! You really can accept things for what they are. It doesn't mean you condone them or that you won't decisively change them; this is about becoming masterful with your mind and your emotional state. It's about quieting the mind and allowing yourself to act with power in the situations of your life rather than succumbing to your internal and external upsets.

## EXPECTING NOTHING, ACCEPTING EVERYTHING

None of this means you can't plan, or that I'm telling you to walk through life aimlessly without direction or goals.

But when you make a plan, what do you have to gain from being welded to the expectations inherent in it? Nothing. When you are free from its expectations you are "in a dance" with life where you can simply execute the plan, and deal with what happens.

If it succeeds, you can celebrate. If it fails, you can recalibrate.

Don't **expect** victory or defeat. Plan for victory, learn from defeat. The expectation of people loving you or respecting you is a pointless exercise, too. Be free to love them the way they are and be loved the way that they love you. Free yourself from the burden and melodrama of expectation; let the chips fall where they may.

Love the life you have, not the one you expected to have.

*"Stay out of
the swamp
of mediocrity
and drama,
reach for your
greatest self,
your greatest
potential, and
challenge
yourself to live
that life every
single day of it."*

"I expect nothing and accept everything." This simple personal assertion gets you out of your head and powerfully into your life, out of your thoughts and into your reality. Problems, barriers, disagreements, and disappointments are all part of every human being's life.

Your job is to not get caught up in that crap, to stay out of the swamp of mediocrity and drama, to reach for your greatest self, your greatest potential, and to challenge yourself to live that life every single day of it.

Your life, your success, your happiness really are in your own hands. The power to change, the power to let go, be adventurous, and embrace your potential all lie within your reach. Remember, no one can save you, no one can shift you, all of that is your responsibility and what better time to embrace that change than now?

# Where next?

"It's this simple: in order to improve your internal world, you have to start by taking action in the external world. Get out of your mind, and get out into your life."

# CHAPTER 9

# I've given you seven personal assertions.

*"I am willing."*

*"I am wired to win."*

*"I got this."*

*"I embrace the uncertainty."*

*"I am not my thoughts; I am what I do."*

*"I am relentless."*

*"I expect nothing and accept everything."*

Each of them plays into a theme. You may not immediately see it, but it's there.

If you want your life to be different, you have to make it happen. All of the thinking or meditating or planning or anti-anxiety medication in the world isn't going to improve your life if you're not willing to go out and take action and make changes. You can't sit around waiting for the right mood to strike or for life to play out the way you want it to. Nor can you rely on positive thinking alone to transform things for the better. You have to go out and **do**.

One of the ironic things about developing our mind and our mindset is that it can actually keep us from acting on the things we really need to act on. You can become a personal development drone. You know tons of cool shit but it's made little or no difference to the trajectory of your life.

We think, "As soon as I get rid of my worry or discomfort, I'll start dating again." Or, "When I find the root of my procrastination or when I find something to motivate me, I'll be completely unleashed and happy." The desire to work on our "procrastination" just leaves us stuck in the cycle of procrastination and not-procrastination and keeps us even further from forwarding our actual lives.

We're waiting on that moment or experience when everything in our mind is just perfect. Our thoughts are clear, our emotions are positive, and our anxiety or worry has completely disappeared.

When we **feel** "off," we put our lives off. That's right, you're waiting on a feeling.

Life doesn't work like that. There is no perfect mood. And while you're waiting on it to improve and miraculously make your life better, eh, guess what? Your life isn't getting any better! None of these assertions are going to make your life easy. Hell, for a while, they're more than likely to make your life harder! Nor is it enough to simply internalize them. You need to **act** on them.

It's this simple: in order to improve your internal world, you have to start by taking action in the external world. Get out of your mind, and get out into your life.

## YOU'RE GOING TO DIE

*"If I take death into my life, acknowledge it, and face it squarely, I will free myself from the anxiety of death and the pettiness of life—and only then will I be free to become myself."*

*- Martin Heidegger*

One day, you're going to die. You're going to stop breathing, become still, and cease to exist. You will exit this physical plane. Whether it's tomorrow or twenty years from now, it's going to happen.

We're all mortal. There's no escaping it. You might find discomfort in these words or resist the notion of your demise but if it's truth you're after, that's the one truth you just cannot argue with. You are going to die.

Imagine that you're on your deathbed. You hear the beep . . . beep . . . beep of the monitor nearby. Your health is critical, and you've only got a few hours to live. You can feel your heartbeat and energy slide.

As you lie there, you start to look back on your life. You never made the change you wanted. You stayed stuck in that same job, that same relationship, that same overweight body until now, the day you die.

You read books, but you never applied them. You planned diets, but you never followed them. You told yourself what you were going to do, psyched yourself up a thousand times, but you never did it. You started dozens if not hundreds of life changing escapades and then wilted.

As you lie there in your hospital bed, loved ones cycling in and out over the course of the day, what do you feel?

Regret? Remorse? Sorrow? What would you give if you could go back to this moment—the one in which you're reading this book—and do things differently? If only . . .

Dammit, WAKE UP! The regret will course through your body, your mind, your heart. It'll be crushing. Unbearable. You're not sure whether to fear death or to welcome it, just so it can take you out of this misery.

Here's the thing: future you is not going to regret a lack of achievement or the absence of any one thing in your life. The only thing you will regret is not trying. Not striving. Not pushing through when the going got tough.

Not all mountaineers make the summit; sometimes they turn back, retool, keep coming at it. They're just never satisfied with standing at the bottom, hanging out with all the other nonclimbers and explaining their lack of ascent. No, they packed up their tent and moved forward, and they will pass from this world knowing they gave every ounce of their effort. That they played full out. They loved the climb.

You won't regret not making a million dollars; you'll regret never starting that business or quitting that lousy job. You won't regret not marrying a supermodel; you'll regret staying in that dead-end relationship when you knew you could do better. You won't regret not looking like a bodybuilder; you'll regret stopping at the drive-thru every night on your way home and living a lie.

And this will happen to you. You will die. You will go through all of that on your own, in the quiet solitude of your own dwindling consciousness.

Unless you take the action that's needed to change, to build the life you want, the life you can be proud of.

## STOP BUYING YOURSELF OFF

We're constantly buying ourselves off. We have all kinds of things we tell ourselves about why we "can't."

I can't, I can't, I can't. But you can. These are all just excuses. You promise yourself all kinds of new actions, you put them off with a litany of reasons and end up with nothing more than a growing relationship to yourself as a bullshitter!

You're way more likely to sell out on yourself than anyone else!

The only difference between you and the person who's living the life you want is that they're doing it. They've built that life, and they're living it.

They're not smarter, more mindful, stronger, or any of that stuff. They don't have anything you don't. The only difference is that successful people don't wait. They're not waiting for the "right" moment. They don't wait for inspiration to strike or for some cosmic event to force them to action. They get up and they do, and they try, and they fail even before they may feel "ready." They're flying the airplane while they're building it. If it falls out of the sky, they'll piece it back together and try again.

Your internal condition means nothing. It's just another excuse that you give yourself to stay out of the risky zones of life. The problem is, those risky zones ARE life! The rest is just existing.

## STOP BLAMING YOUR PAST

For those of you who are blaming your past, thinking that holds you back, I invite you to think again. I invite you to confront the notion that what has been is greater than what can be. We all have pasts; some of them are fucking horrific. SO WHAT!!!!????? Before you jump furiously on the offended bus, why is it you show more passion for your past than you do for your future? You and I both know no one can free you but you. I'm not just another guy in the diner with an opinion; I've coached people with pasts that would make your toes curl. They have gone on to live free and happy lives and you can, too.

People become trapped in their past, trapped in their childhood. It's one of the many reasons we tell ourselves that we "can't." It's an easy way to relieve yourself of the responsibility you have for your current circumstances.

But nothing can stop you from moving forward and being great, if that's what you really want. It doesn't matter what happened yesterday or five years ago or when you were in second grade.

Just like how we improve our internal by moving to the external, we can forget our past by creating a future. Build something big, something bigger than anything you've done.

When what's in front of you is so bright and so satisfying, you won't have time to look behind you.

Your eyes and mind will be focused straight ahead.

That will draw you out. A big enough, bright enough, sexy enough future, a future so soaked with potential and possibility its weight will snap you free from that significant and laborious past.

You may not like everything from your past, but it's helped shape who you are today, good and bad. That's right, there is plenty good about you, and that good is enough to get you what you want. That person is fully capable of living the life they want. Nothing will hold you back, if you want it enough and act on it enough.

## TWO STEPS TO FREEDOM

If you're truly ready to change your life, to take hold of that freedom you've been missing, there are two things you need to do.

### 1. Stop doing what you're currently doing.

Simple, right? Look at the things that are sourcing your problems, the habits that have put you in the situation you are in.

If you don't get anything done because you're glued to the couch, binge-watching Netflix for hours at a time, or have become a little too attracted to the delicacies of your local Dunkin Donuts, stop doing it. No, seriously, STOP. Now.

Don't start listing all the reasons you can't. "But the shows are so good, and I'm so tired after work," or "I need the small pleasures to keep me going."

If you can't even stop watching TV long enough to get your life together, you obviously don't want to change. That's basic shit. It's the bare minimum, to be honest.

So what will it be? Netflix or a better paying career? Donuts or a body you can be proud of? Video games or a loving relationship?

If eating out every day makes you feel like crap, why are you still doing it?

And every time you think you "can't" stop, that's just another excuse. You can. You can, and you will. Stop buying yourself off. Stop letting your internal condition dominate the quality of your life. Take back the wheel.

If you continue to be led by your emotions, you'll only be left with regret. You'll eventually live that vision, lying on your deathbed and thinking, "What if?" I'm not saying your emotions and feelings aren't important; I'm not asking you to turn into a robot. What I AM saying is you need to get those experiences much further down the ladder of importance and act on what is going to make the biggest difference to your life.

One of the common excuses we feed ourselves is "I want to change my life but..." while watching hours of TV, eating junk food, reaming our way through Facebook, etc. Be straight with yourself.

YOU DON'T WANT TO CHANGE! If you did, you'd be doing it! Call yourself out on this shit.

Take a long, hard look at your life. Be honest with yourself, identify the behaviors that are holding you back. You need to use every waking hour of your life to further your cause, no excuses. You're not any different or any worse off than anyone else. You're not a fucking special case who needs different rules than everyone else.

You need to make a choice, right now. You're never going to change your life until you get rid of those things. No more excuses.

## 2. Start taking the actions to propel you forward.

Again, pretty straightforward, right? Changing your life isn't just about NOT doing certain things. You've also got to put in the work and build the positive habits that will pull you in the right direction.

If you want a new job, go out and apply for one. Get out there and network. Search the classifieds, talk to friends, ask for references.

No, I mean really do them. Don't say you will, and then don't. Don't hype yourself up, then push it off until tomorrow.

> *"You are what you do, not what you say you'll do."*
> *– Carl Jung*

Take stock of the things you want to achieve. What do you want to accomplish? What do you need to do to get there? Map out the next step—hold yourself accountable, moment by moment by moment, to those steps.

These two steps, stopping and starting, are naturally linked. Because, psychologically, it's hard to just quit something "cold turkey." Especially when it's an addictive habit that affects the very chemistry of our brains, like food or sex or drugs or video games.

Stopping your bad habit doesn't help, unless you replace it with something else, something that actually works in your favor and is an example of the new kind of life you really want to live. It's about systematically replacing the old with the new, forging a new life for yourself—the kind of life you've always wanted.

You have to clear out the bad to make room for the good. Otherwise you're not going to have enough evidence for that new life. You're building a case for a new life, item by item. The process has to be thorough and decisive or you'll always be held back and slowed down on your journey to change, carrying that dead weight.

Quit the TV, the sea of self-help books that you read and do nothing with, excessive eating, sofa camping, and procrastination. Replace them with tango classes, book clubs, eating for fuel, bicycle riding, and expressing yourself . . . ANYTHING!

Need support? Get yourself a coach, a good one, the best you can afford. If money's an issue, join my i365 program, a twelve-month journey of personal expansion and power. It's on my website and you can participate for less than the cost of a daily cup of coffee. Like I said, NO EXCUSES!

## GET OUT OF YOUR HEAD

*"Take time to deliberate, but when the time for action comes, stop thinking and go in."*
– Napoleon Bonaparte

There's a time for thinking and developing your mind. But ultimately you've got to step up to the plate and put what you know into action.

All of your assertions play into that. You are willing—to take action. And to embrace the uncertainty that comes along with it.

"I am relentless" doesn't mean relentlessly thinking or watching TV. It means relentlessly doing. Relentlessly taking action, pursuing your goals, acting and failing and ultimately succeeding.

Nothing that I've shown you will make a single difference in your life, unless you act on it. You have to **make** the difference. Make it happen.

*"This isn't just about seizing the day; this is about seizing the moment, the hour, the week, the month."*

You have to claim your greatness. I'm not going to do it for you. Neither is your mother or your spouse or your neighbor. Confidence won't save you, the future is not suddenly going to improve, your worry isn't going to suddenly disappear, and your new qualifications aren't going to suddenly make you assertive or credible. Only you can take a stand for your potential.

Don't just read this; think about it, and then go on about your life doing the same shit over and over. Apply it.

"I'll do it later"—no, do it now.

"I'm not smart enough to do that"—cut it out. Stop honoring that shit and act.

Don't let your mind control you any longer. Stop letting it hold you back with its excuses and distractions and worries.

You are not your thoughts. You are your actions. You are what you do.

And your actions are the only thing separating you from where you are and where you want to be.

This isn't just about seizing the day; this is about seizing the moment, the hour, the week, the month. This is about seizing your fucking life and staking a claim for yourself as though your life depended on it.

Because, the reality is, it does.

## ABOUT THE AUTHOR

# GARY JOHN BISHOP

Born and raised in Glasgow, Scotland, Gary moved to the United States in 1997. This opened up his pathway to the world of personal development, specifically to ontology and phenomenology, in which he was rigorously trained for a number of years before becoming a senior program director with one of the world's leading personal development companies. After years of facilitating programs to thousands of people all over the world and later studying and being influenced by the philosophies of Martin Heidegger, Hans-Georg Gadamer, and Edmund Husserl, Gary is producing his own brand of "urban philosophy." His lifelong commitment to shifting people's ability to exert real change in their lives drives him each and every day. He has a no-frills, no-bullshit approach that has brought him an ever increasing following, drawn to the simplicity and real-world use of his work. He resides in Florida with his wife and three sons.

## CONNECT

@GARYJOHNBISHOP

GARYJOHNBISHOP.com